4.3.78

FILM IN SWEDEN

The New Directors

Lena Nyman in I AM CURIOUS—YELLOW

FILM IN SWEDEN

The New Directors

by Stig Björkman

Translated by Barrie Selman

London: The Tantivy Press
South Brunswick and New York: A.S. Barnes & Co.
in Collaboration with the Swedish Film Institute and the Swedish Institute, Stockholm

Published in English by

The Tantivy Press
136-148 Tooley Street
London SE1 2TT, England

and

A.S. Barnes & Co.
Cranbury
New Jersey 08512

Cover design by Stefan Dreja

SERIES EDITORS:
Jörn Donner
Peter Cowie

Library of Congress Catalogue Card Number: 75-30229

ISBN 0-498-01863-6 (U.S.A.)
ISBN 0-904208-06-0 (U.K.)

Printed in the United States of America

Contents

1 Foreword

The Swedish film reform was carried out in 1963. On July 1 of that year the 25% entertainments tax, which had previously been imposed on the price of cinema tickets, was removed. In its place a 10% charge was introduced, the revenue from which is deposited in a fund administered by the Swedish Film Institute.

The money which thus came under the control of the Film Institute — amounting over the first few years to an annual sum of about ten to twelve million kronor — was shared out among five different funds:

A (30%) for reimbursement to Swedish film production, a sum commensurate with the gross box-office takings of the film being repaid to the producer.

B (20%) for quality grants, a sum in accordance with an expert film jury's assessment of the current year's Swedish films.

C (15%) as a subsidy to cover the losses on these quality award-winning productions.

D (5%) for publicity work for Swedish films.

E (30%) for research, tuition and administration, i.e. for the film archives (films, books, pictures, documentation), the restoration of historically valuable films, and to the newly established film school for the training of directors, cameramen, sound technicians and production managers.

So after years of hesitation and indifference the Swedish state had, by this — admittedly limited — financial initiative, accepted some measure of responsibility for a sector of cultural life which had long been neglected. The film reform signified a step forward, a sort of official recognition of the cinema as an art form, and an attempt to revitalise a business which had lapsed into a more or less acute state of crisis and — with a few exceptions — was distinguished by only one internationally famous artist, Ingmar Bergman.

The film reform brought about a vital transformation and renewal of the Swedish cinema, and the latter half of the Sixties was marked by optimism and activity. Something like thirty Swedish feature films were produced annually; during the ten years following the introduction of the film reform about sixty new film-makers made their *début,* and nearly a dozen feature films were produced by various film co-operatives.

The Sixties were a dynamic period for the Swedish cinema, and its more progressive representatives gave new life to an art form which for a long time had been hobbling along on crutches. The new directors pointed the way towards new production forms and towards cheaper, simplified and more rational shooting methods. They abandoned the fusty atmosphere and synthetic dream world of the film studios, coming closer to reality and more substantial visions, something which the Swedish cinema had been avoiding for years. Bo Widerberg gave the starting signal with *The Pram,* and he had many followers, especially among the collective productions made during the close of the decade.

This increase in output was accompanied by a simultaneous development of the trade union movement within the cinema. Film workers finally started to get organised. They started consciously working for better conditions, both financial and political. Film workers made demands for greater co-determination within their professional field and within the Swedish Film Institute, but soon found that they were being opposed by the establishment in the form of the Film Institute and its allies, the Swedish film industry.

The wider aspirations of the film workers in the sphere of film politics were also demonstrated by the formation of Film Centrum, an association which by means of active distribution outside the commercial system seeks to spread the films of its members. Film Centrum also tries, despite very limited resources and mainly through the individual support of its members, to encourage the production of more political and socially orientated films, a type of film which the film business after a few half-hearted projects now seems to have eschewed. Film Centrum has also taken much of the initiative in building up trade union consciousness and activity.

The dynamic effects of the film reform were not lasting. By the beginning of the Seventies the number of feature films produced per year had declined to something like fifteen. Many voices were raised in favour of alterations and improvements of the film subsidy, a reduction of business influence of Swedish film production and policy, and the nationalisation of the cinema.

The agreement reached between the state and the film industry in 1963 was in fact modified in many essential respects in 1972. The fund system had formerly been constructed in such a way that the film subsidy was awarded retrospectively, that is to feature films which had already been produced and distributed. This involved a consider-able risk for those seeking to produce films, and especially to the free film producers with no distribution channels of their own and therefore in greater need of this subsidy.

What now occurred was a re-distribution of resources. Three new funds were set up, while the earlier funds for retroactive subsidies were greatly reduced in favour of advance subsidies and the direct financing of film productions. There is now an F fund, which grants a direct guarantee subsidy to all Swedish feature films; a G fund, which finances the Film Institute's own production of shorts and feature films; and two H funds, H1 and H2, which allocate project subsidies (grants for screenplay work and research) and direct production guarantees "to films with an artistic purpose and aiming at a wide public." The intention was to create a pluralistic system. The H funds, for example, have been divided up in such a way that one of the funds is headed by representatives of the commercial film business, while the other recruits its members from the various cinema trade unions. In addition the state has allocated a small sum of money every year (at present a couple of million kronor) to these funds. It is estimated that within a few years these funds will be capable of covering 60-65% of the production costs of a film.

This subsidy structure is virtually unique in the West — only Denmark and Canada are able to show any similar alternatives. But what continues to bedevil and weaken the Swedish system is the dependence of the Film Institute and of film policy on the commercial film business.

Like so much else in Swedish economic life, the situation of the cinema is marked by incomplete and irresolute political initiatives. The Swedish cinema is stuck in a deadlock between big business on the one hand, and, on the other, a professed readiness to assist on the part of the government which the latter has failed to fulfill. The socialist idea of equality, which is present as an underlying outlook, has not been translated into reality.

Widerberg's closing words in *Ådalen 31* could be applied directly to the situation of the Swedish cinema today.

Both in its earliest and also in its present, modified form, the film reform is chiefly adapted to the cinema picture and the needs of the business. The business contributes its tithe, but is thus able to wield an influence on the Swedish cinema which corresponds neither to its knowledge nor its responsibility.

The theatre is subsidised in Sweden to the tune of eighty or ninety million kronor annually. The cinema receives a couple of million in direct grants. True, the conditions have been created for a film production which could offer continuity and variety. But since the business — despite its financial and material resources and notwithstanding the considerable support provided out of the Film Institute's funds — continues to pursue a passive production policy, the state ought to involve itself in the cinema in a more active way, break with the wrong and restricting dependence on the business and assume the responsibility in the form of financial subsidies which a measure like this necessitates. Such subsidies should have more realistic proportions than at present (and this applied not only to film production but also to distribution, and to aid to the film archives and research); and they should also bear some relation to the grants which the rest of the arts receive.

"It would be a good thing if we could reach agreement about the things which we ought to have in common: continued de-commercialisation, a definition of the cinema's function in society, an environment which stimulates the development of the cinematic language — regardless of the uses to which this language is put," wrote Harry Schein recently, the architect of the film reform and the head of the Film Institute from the start. In this spirit the Film Institute and official film policy should enter into alliance with the film workers and their interests.

For behind the films which could be created with the aid of a progressively larger and more active subsidisation there are the film-makers, staking their work, their know-how, their ideas, their dreams, their involvement, their belief in the cinema as a manifestation of culture and as an intellectual or political or emotional weapon.

This book is about some of them. It is a look back. The essays might have been greater in number and included more names. But this is, above all, not a history of the cinema but just an extract from it. And there is a group of talents who can and will carry on where it leaves off.

Inger Taube in THE PRAM

2 New Images and Daylight

It is no exaggeration to say that the new Swedish cinema was initiated by Bo Widerberg. He became its first and most influential spokesman. With his earliest films he provided its first examples. They pointed the way towards a freer film style, a way out of the stereotype pattern of the commercial Swedish cinema with its technically proficient but non-committal factory products, in which "mediocrity is raised to a landmark and fictitious problems are presented in a pseudo-world mendaciously called Sweden," to quote Widerberg himself.

In 1962 — at the same time as he was directing his first film, *The Pram* — Widerberg published a polemical book entitled "Vision in the Swedish Cinema." Vision is the technical term in Swedish for the slow transition from one shot to another, and vision is also employed here as a symbol of the author's demand for radical renewal.

The view of the cinema which Widerberg advocates in this book is that of a cinema learning how to spell *reality.* He formulates the desire for a more subtle differentiation of the picture of Sweden which must emerge in films set and shot here. A cinema which does not falsify and distort reality in a cardboard world but presents it in a new and truer light. His book also pleaded for a new style of filming, for a cheaper and less cumbersome production technique, and a set of aesthetics adapted to this necessity. A cinema seeking — and finding — its usefulness and justification outside the conventional profitability calculations of the film industry.

Widerberg's models were the French *nouvelle vague* — Truffaut, Demy, Godard; recent American films such as Paddy Chayefsky's realistic everyday dramas, and above all John Cassavetes's *Shadows;* and the English cinema as represented by Karel Reisz's *Saturday Night and Sunday Morning.* "Films which show not only the conflicts of their characters but also their material conditions, how they live, what they eat, and where they work, and tackling the issues of human dignity and responsibility in their proper human environment."

With *The Pram,* Widerberg proved his thesis. The film was made at the very low production cost of 200,000 kronor, on location in Malmö. Widerberg gave the leading role to an amateur, a photographic model called Inger Taube (possibly inspired by Godard's successful collaboration with Anna Karina), and the other parts to then comparatively unknown actors.

The Pram is a film with a good deal of feeling, atmosphere, intimacy — and many flaws. Not unexpectedly it was greeted with rather harsh criticism. People had attuned their expectations and demands to Widerberg's tartly formulated manifesto.

The Pram roped in a chunk of Swedish reality. It was made with inquisitiveness and enthusiasm. But the explorative gusto and pioneering spirit which pervade the film still cannot disguise a number of its dramatical and formal flaws.

In *The Pram* Widerberg sought to answer some of the questions which he believed the contemporary Swedish cinema all too often evaded: Where do you live? What do you do during the day? What do you do at night? What do you talk about during the coffee break? Do you have an idea which makes it easier/harder for you to live with others?

The main character, Britt, is drifting around in life. She has no firm foothold anywhere. Certainly not in her work. She soon tires of the dull jobs to

Thommy Berggren and Inger Taube in THE PRAM

which she is restricted by her poor education, and leaves when she finds the routine suffocating. Still living at home, she is dutifully tied to her mother and aloof towards her younger brother. She has no steady boyfriend but lets herself get picked up when she feels in the mood. Her erotic encounters take place in the dilapidated entrance hall of the block of flats where she lives, and are very much dependent on whether or not they are disturbed by the neighbours. She swaps secrets with her workmates during the breaks or visits to the toilet, but she does not seem to mix with her girlfriends in her spare time.

Britt's situation is undoubtedly typical of that of many young women in all its pathetic bareness.

The Pram is one of the first attempts to portray a woman in modern Swedish cinema. And in the picture of Britt lie the chief merits of the film. There are no romantic palliatives, no glamorisation. Neither is there any specious or patronising sentimentality. Britt is not forced to be any different from what she is really like. She is allowed to voice her opinions directly — or rather to reveal her life right there in front of the camera. For Britt is a human being who has no language. This is her greatest dilemma.

Rather carelessly, Britt becomes pregnant. But the father, a young musician, soon vanishes from the scene, and Britt formulates her first independent decision: her intention to keep the baby and care for it herself.

The Pram describes a maturing process. By her decision Britt gives content to her aimless life. By making herself responsible for her actions she also accepts responsibility for herself. Her life acquires a meaning.

Britt meets another young man. He is quite unlike her earlier boyfriends. He is sensitive, well read, and has a greater verbal capacity for expressing himself. He befriends Britt in a paternal way, and she is attracted by his mixture of confidence and gentleness. He tries to bring her knowledge and culture, hoping at the same time through Britt to emerge a few steps from his world of caution and refinement, and acquire experiences of a more primitive or immediate nature. In this he is no exception to his class. He gives of himself and his abundance, but with the ulterior motive, no doubt unconscious, of reaping benefits for himself. But the man is much too tied to his environment, suffering above all from a strong mother fixation, to be able to offer any real support. In a decisive situation he lets her down.

But Britt is able to endure this betrayal. It cannot make her swerve from the path she has laid out for herself. This is where her maturity becomes evident.

The closing scenes of The Pram radiate affirmation and optimism but without any romantic discolouring. Britt is pushing her pram along open, bright, sunlit streets. The windows on the way throw back flashing reflexions. Britt walks alone, but this is not a journey through the sweet masochism of self-sacrifice. Britt has achieved independence and awareness. She realises that her place in life is not static.

With The Pram Widerberg attempted to break with the formalism of the commercial Swedish cinema. He sought to develop a realism expressing itself in the depiction of realistic action and realistic points of view.

The Pram takes up the struggle against the creations of the commercial cinema and the problems it deals with, against those archetypes and paper constructions of the cinema which move across the screen in a stiff, ceremonious manner, performing actions of purely formal value.

The Swedish cinema had too long neglected to illuminate the more all-round development of man. It treated its characters in a conservative way, i.e. as if locked up in classes and values. To the extent that such films described personal development it was generally in the form of the ennobling of the individual within a very limited and complacent context. Love and faith were the only issues considered worthy of a thorough-going portrayal (as in Bergman's films, for example). At times directors might pretend to espouse more progressive viewpoints by locating the drama in a working class setting. But the story would never free itself from what was predestined. No matter how evocative or sweaty or muscular the treatment might be. It always moved within the formalism and tradition of the commercial cinema. Human behaviour was determined by the material conditions which an unchangeable society has to offer. And the outlook of the commercial Swedish cinema has always been conservative.

The Pram marks a break with this formalism. It applies a plasticity to its depiction of its characters. Widerberg uses a montage technique — not in order to simplify the picture of Britt but to give it depth and complexity. Where there is a reason for simply indicating a sequence of events — because it is too familiar or or of general validity — Widerberg abbreviates it with a few rapid cuts. Where there is a reason for stopping and listening to the characters, Widerberg allows himself and his actors plenty of time.

The method employed by Widerberg can be more effective than emerges from *The Pram.* There is much about the film that seems haphazard and incomplete. The application is still too vague and whimsical, and the action of the film makes sudden twists that catch it off balance. Sometimes one wishes that the camera had dwelt longer on the characters, while elsewhere there are unnecessary *longueurs.* Yet *The Pram* provides an example of an effective method, which Widerberg has elected to follow up and develop in a more conscious fashion in his subsequent films.

* * *

"Do you know why I make films?...Am I talking too much?

"What has happened to the cinema is that it has gone and got a morality. It has at last had the courage to show that it is just cinema and nothing else. 'A film,' says Godard, 'is the truth twenty-four times a second.' He cannot commit himself further than that. And for Antonioni every choice of camera angle is a question of morality. . .

"It's no longer possible to make films two hours long, with a beginning, a middle and an end. The old film was a lie even in its very form. It laid claim to continuity, to being unbroken. It told of a world which was whole and unbroken and could be interpreted in one way only. Where is that world today?

"Am I giving a lecture?

"No, the truth about today cannot be stretched out lengthwise. The artist cannot come along with bits of a puzzle any more, because there is no pattern to put together. What we can do is to lay the pieces on top of each other and hold them up to the light. And then, if we can detect a pattern, it may perhaps be the truth, or at least a small part of it. . ."

These are the words of the film director Keve, one of the main characters in *Love 65.*

Love 65 is a film about freedom. It is about freedom in art and freedom between people. About freedom as a dream and freedom as pain. *Love 65* is an expression of freedom, and is also Widerberg's most open and easily accessible film. *Love 65* bids us welcome to a lovingly prepared meal, and we enter the film expectantly, in a festive mood.

Love 65 is also a film about seeing.

In one of the first scenes in the film Keve and the actress Inger arrive at Keve's house in the country, where his wife Ann-Mari and little daughter Nina live. (The little girl is played by Widerberg's daughter Nina, who took part in all of his earlier films.)

Inger Taube in THE PRAM

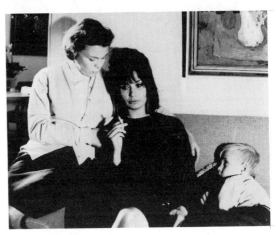

At home with mother

Nina has been drawing pictures of her parents and their friends, and after they have admired her pictures, Inger suddenly asks her why she wears such strange glasses. One of the lenses is lacquered. Nina invites Inger to look for herself; she has a severe squint, but when Inger holds her hand over the girl's right eye, the left eye looks straight ahead. When Inger moves her hand over to the left eye, Nina's right eye quickly compensates and now looks straight ahead at Inger.

Nina is a camera, as are Keve, Inger and the rest of the characters in the film. (Widerberg sometimes narrows down his characters' field of vision in this way, as if to stress that they themselves can alter the limits of their perception, and thus of their action, too. An instance of this is in the long dialogue scene between Inger and Ann-Mari in the outdoor toilets at the fairground. They are sitting on opposite sides of a wooden partition, and are able to focus each other through a knot-hole.)

Ann-Mari explains that it is possible to operate on Nina's squint. She had to have such an operation herself when she was young. It does not

hurt, but you have a bandage over your eyes for five days. What is frightening is the dark. "Do you realise what it is you see in there in the dark? Everything you have ever experienced up to then, everything you have experienced at home. Everything that exists around you goes on existing in there. And gets bigger. . ."

Widerberg describes the film director as a *voyeur.* Keve wanders through life observing the people closest to him. His wife, his daughter, his friends. Perhaps one day he may be able to use something they have to contribute in one of his films. A gesture, a look, an expression.

Keve quite shamelessly seduces a young woman, Evabritt, right in front of her husband. Without so much as a word or a gesture, but with a look so full of longing and desire that no words are strong enough to pit against it in protest or resistance.

It is at one of his love meetings with Evabritt that Keve talks about the morality and truth of the cinema. He is playing around with a view-finder, a lens through which it is possible to study and determine the framing of the subject in front of the camera. It is the instrument of artistic creation and freedom. He demonstrates it to Evabritt. There are no limits to what they can create.

This is where the poetry in *Love 65* springs from, poetry in its ability to give with unique power voice or image to the instinctive emotional processes occurring inside every human being. Poetry stands opposed to all that makes demands on one. Duty and social conflicts are kept at a distance, balanced by poetry deriving its sustenance from the pleasures of life — love, joy, fellowship. Evabritt's and Keve's erotic meetings in the empty flat are depicted with a sensual heat and intensity which few Swedish films can equal. Embraces, voyages of exploration, observations at the meeting-place that is love.

The greater part of *Love 65* is set in and around a summer-house in southern Sweden. There live Keve, Ann-Mari and Nina, and Inger is their guest. They are joined by Ben Carruthers, the actor from *Shadows.* He is to appear in Keve's new film.

But the days slip by in idleness. They cook food and fly kites on the hills by the sea. *Love 65* describes a creative crisis similar to that of *8½,* but without the anguish emanating from Fellini's film. Keve's dilemma is less neurotic. He feels an aversion for the new film and lacks ideas. His thoughts soar as high as the kites, and like Prometheus, Keve seems to be trying to win back the lost fire from the gods. But in the next scene we see him sleeping peacefully, while the kite fastened to his belt still strives upwards, unconcerned about its owner.

Freedom also implies a freedom from creating. One lives according to a feeling and accepts it. This may be called living poetically, but this attitude is a luxury, and whoever chooses to live in this way runs the risk of being misunderstood or deserted.

Inger Taube, Keve Hjelm and Ann-Mari Gyllenspetz in LOVE 65

Love 65 breathes peace, light and purity. The characters move through open landscapes and rooms almost carved out of glass. But beneath the calm, unruffled surface there are vulnerable spots and conflicts. Keve's and Ann-Mari's marriage is not a happy one. There is a wary suspiciousness in their encounters. Ann-Mari is obliged to perform her creative acts in the home, and cannot allow herself the same liberties as Keve. This gives rise to bitterness and distrust, which increase with Keve's refusal to accept responsibility for what they have in common, their daughter. "When do you ever care about Nina? — except when you want her in one of your damn films!" At the same time Keve is irritated by Ann-Mari's passivity, by her feeling of inferiority for not working. "Christ, if only she could get herself a girlfriend. Someone to run me down to!"

The appealing thing about Widerberg in *Love 65* is that he does not fight shy of the complications occurring in human relationships. *Love 65* might have turned out as merely a romantic and sensual account of a poetic life. (Compare it with *Elvira Madigan,* or with *Joe Hill,* which is a romantic and sensual account of a political life.) But Widerberg delves beneath the specious, languid surface and exposes the underlying conflicts.

This is not done in a dramatically explicit or straightforward manner. Widerberg creates few situations which openly air people's aggressions. The knots binding his characters are laid bare in a more subtle way. They engage almost confidentially in the conversations which comprise *one* of

the mainstays of the film. I write "confidentially" because not even during these conversations are the problems posed openly. Widerberg expects, or hopes, that the contact which we have acquired with the roles is strong (and friendly) enough for us, the audience, to grasp even confidences imparted in a throw-away phrase.

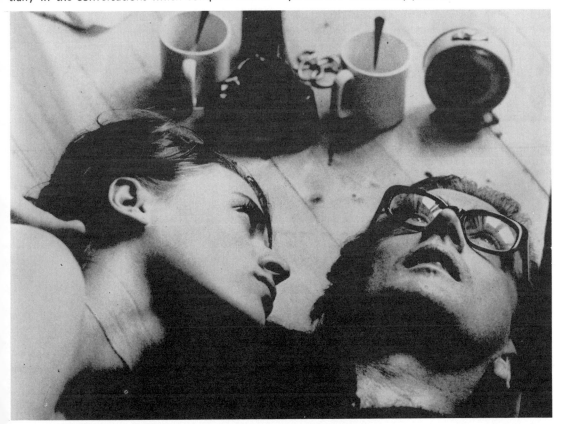

Keve Hjelm as the film director with his mistress (Evabritt Strandberg)

Here lies the secret of Widerberg's method of deploying his actors. Widerberg seeks to avoid anything that might be termed "acting." He does not look for miming and emphasis. He seeks to root the roles in the actors and elicit a spontaneous personal response from them. This is why the actors ring truer when they are permitted to talk directly to each other than when they are subjected to a dramatic conflict steered from without. All of Widerberg's films are constructed around this sort of verbal confession of profound intimacy which enables the actors to motivate their parts and bring them closer to the audience.

"My entire acting principle amounts to letting the actors use one another," Widerberg has said. "One ploughs the other's field, and vice versa. It is also a moral principle that no-one shall get up and try to outdo the other and create a character profile all on his own. You must rely on the person whom you are looking in the eye. Nothing else must arise except for what springs from this connection — unless, of course, the scene requires that something else should emerge."

In *Love 65* Widerberg has gone so far — not in the actors' identification with their parts, but in the director's identification with the actors — that the actors retain their own names in the fictitious film drama. They also contribute characteristics from their real lives. Thus, for example, when Ann-Mari is talking to Ben Carruthers about his experiences from *Shadows* she is probably asking as much in her capacity of Ann-Mari Gyllenspetz as in her role as the wife of Keve the film director.

Love 65 is also the film that is most faithful to Widerberg's aesthetic principles. Widerberg renounces any kind of artificiality. Daylight washes in over the images, imbuing them with a clean pictorial beauty. And the actors have sufficiently strong personalities to be able to assert themselves in this lighting. The tempo of the montage, the musicality, match perfectly the pulse of the action.

Love 65 strikes a balance between *The Pram,* in which the images are so bare in expression that only odd scenes are capable of challenging our emotions; and *Elvira Madigan,* in which the images are so fraught with beauty that our emotions are almost raped. *Love 65* is Widerberg's most harmonious film. It is like a clear and refreshing spring.

* * *

Widerberg's film work almost has the character of crop-rotation. *Motifs,* methods and *milieux* are dropped and then re-cycled. It is possible to link up Widerberg's films in pairs. *The Pram* and *Love 65* represent a common line, as regards *motif* and form, and they most clearly demonstrate Widerberg's fundamental ambition: the desire to confront the viewer with human conflicts and responsibilities in a setting that is firmly anchored in reality. The two comedies in a present-day setting, *Thirty Times Your Money* and *Stubby,* show Widerberg as a strained and breathless entertainer.

Thirty Times Your Money is based on a novel by Widerberg called "The Green Kite," which describes farcical adventures in the advertising business. But both in the book and in the film the dialogue feels forced and the situations contrived. Neither do the actors, who seem to have been directed with book in hand, manage to find a method of making the plot in any way amusing.

Stubby is the story of a seven-year-old footballer who runs rings round the Sweden centre-forward and then goes on to take his place in the Swedish team and salvage the national honour in the World Cup. Widerberg squeezes this brilliant idea dry until all the charm and arch absurdity are lost. The joke is repeated, and the film's professional actors indulge in vaudeville apparently unchecked by the director, who seems to cherish the naïve hope that we are willing to let ourselves be surprised over and over again *ad infinitum*. Humour is probably the weakest point in Widerberg's professional temperament.

Widerberg's "historical" films can also be divided up. *Raven's End* and *Ådalen 31* are carried along by similar themes. They attempt to re-establish a sense of affinity with historical origins. They depict the liberation of the individual in a struggle which is as much concerned with the personal as with the collective.

Thommy Berggren and Pia Degermark go to their death in ELVIRA MADIGAN

Elvira Madigan and *Joe Hill* are mirrors of dreams — dreams of love and justice. One expresses emotions in a historical period but outside a social situation *(Elvira Madigan);* the other, emotions in a historical period but within a social situation and a political context *(Joe Hill).*

Elvira Madigan, Sixten Sparre and Joe Hill — as they emerge from Widerberg's films — have a lot in common. They are romantics and rebels, defying established society and its norms. They are pioneers, battling for values which society attempts to suppress. All of them evince a longing to excape the oppression of the *bourgeoisie.* With Elvira and Sixten it assumes the form of flight back to a primitive life. With Joe Hill it leads to struggle. The heroes of the two films perish — through their own stringent demands and the resistance of society. *Elvira Madagan* and *Joe Hill* are tragedies, but the tragedy is not tragic in itself — it is beautiful and tender and offers purification. *Elvira Madigan* and *Joe Hill* are two optimistic tragedies.

Above: ELVIRA MADIGAN

Both *Elvira Madagan* and *Joe Hill* are sentimental journeys back to the landscapes of the emotions where these people lived and were sacrificed. In both of these nostalgic voyages Widerberg equates sensualism with realism, realism being not the fruit of study and methodical observation but of a more immediate experience. He makes the same intuitive documentation of a period and a train of events in *Raven's End* and *Ådalen 31.*

* * *

The narrative of *Raven's End* commences on May Day, 1936. The date was not picked at random. The film depicts a working-class family in Malmö. By choosing May Day Widerberg underlines his solidarity with the labour movement. Social Democracy has a couple of years behind it as the party of government, and the foundations of social equality and the welfare state are being laid. 1936 is also the fateful year in which Nazism is gaining an ever firmer footing and impressing its monopoly of power on the world consciousness, aided by the great propaganda exercise at the summer Olympics in Berlin. 1936 is the year of the Spanish Civil War. These threats from without make sporadic intrusions into the account of Raven's End and its occupants.

Widerberg has said that he got the idea for the film one day when he went with his father to a place just outside Malmö to fetch some sand for his father's cat. In his head Widerberg heard a mother say to her grown-up son: "I could never look after you during the best years." This line recurs in the film:

MOTHER: What makes me sad is that I never had
the time to look after you when you were
small. . . The best time. . . Not that you were
much to. . . That's how it's always been for
the likes of us. Making kids is the pleasure of

Thommy Berggren as the young writer in RAVEN'S END

the poor, so they say. What a pleasure — when you can't afford to *enjoy* them!

In its setting, its characters, its action, in fact in every scene, *Raven's End* shows its loyalty to a class. It is an expression of class consciousness and class struggle. *Raven's End* is a belated attempt to document an age. The Swedish cinema of the Thirties consisted almost exclusively of drawing-room comedies and love-melodramas in upperclass interiors knocked up in the property workshop. *Raven's End* comes to terms with former omissions and provides a perspective. It bridges the gap with the present, and creates understanding for it by returning to origins.

Anders, the main character in *Raven's End*, also wishes to describe this period and these people in this block. He dreams of becoming a writer, and in the evenings when all is quiet in the house he works on his novel.

MOTHER: What's it about then?

ANDERS: It's about us.

FATHER: About us? Mum and me?

ANDERS: Well, no not just about you... About the whole block. I'm describing what it's like for us — that's all. How the hell will they ever realise what things are like for us — if we just go on keeping quiet about it? Never mind that they stop us getting a proper education and places fit to live in — but as long as they let us go on calling our peritonitis "gut-ache" we've got every right to shout loud enough for them to hear. And they're going to hear all right — the ones who can afford to call the doctor as soon as their kids get a fart stuck up their ass-holes.

And he sends the novel to a publisher's in Stockholm. One day Anders gets a letter and a train ticket. They are interested in his book. Perhaps they are planning to publish it. Anders's departure for Stockholm is as triumphant as his homecoming is ignominious. Even in this sphere, which he believed to be above making such distinctions, Anders feels himself to be a victim of class antagonisms. The rather patronising benevolence of the publishers makes Anders feel his lack of education, his lack of words.

ANDERS: They just snapped their fingers, and I came. Then they just snapped their fingers again and sent me back home again. There I sat in my Sunday best... It wasn't supposed to be a fashion show, was it? ...But aren't you going to publish it? I said. Oh no, it had

never crossed their minds. But there was something about it which made them want to encourage me to keep it up. There was a cry in it — those were his very words... there was a cry in it which was unarticulated as yet...

MOTHER: Unarticulated — what's that?

ANDERS: It's... It's when you shout so loud that nobody hears what you're saying.

Widerberg is not didactic when it comes to conveying the life of these people. It is not founded on any firm or explicit sense of political fellowship. Anders's mother and father have reaped too much bitterness — his father drinks and does odd jobs when he can get them, while his mother takes in washing to earn enough to keep the family — to be able to appreciate solidarity as a political argument. It is something that simply exists and is taken for granted. When Anders tries to persuade his mother to go and vote she sees it as pointless and irrelevant. "Another vote more or less — what difference does it make?" Yet she goes to the polling station and, refusing the voting slip offered her by the Nazi party, drops the slip marked Labour Party into the envelope and seals it up.

Raven's End describes an act of departure. In the final scenes Anders leaves home, but his departure is not the outcome of a run-of-the-mill revolt against his parents. The positive thing about the film is that while following the path towards maturity and awareness which the film describes, Anders realises that his struggle is identical with his parents' striving for a better life. By leaving them he is not only better able to assert himself but also to summon up sufficient strength to take action to improve his parents' life. This is why he regards it as a threat, or as a corrupt attempt at persuasion which he is not even prepared to answer, when his mother tries to get him to stay for the sake of Elsie, the girl he has made pregnant. Anders leaves her behind, along with a

The march sets out in ÅDALEN 31

life together with her in the flat across the yard which is soon to be vacant. For he is convinced that his way out can also mean the way out for all of them.

Anders has seen and experienced how life has weakened and enslaved his parents. On May Day, when the film opens, his mother is standing in the kitchen ironing football shirts. His father has got an odd job delivering advertising leaflets. But later when Anders goes to the match, he finds his father boozing with his mates in the middle of the crowd which is acclaiming the home team's goalscorer.

Back home mother serves up diced pork and salad — or pork *noisette jardinière* as his father prefers to call it. Mother talks about the fireworks they are going to see in the evening, and father settles down on the sofa for an after-dinner nap. When mother goes to hang up father's jacket she finds that the pockets are full of the undelivered leaflets. Evening comes, and the fireworks illuminate *Raven's End*. There lies father, still fast asleep on the sofa. Mother is glimpsed hurrying into the entrance of a block of flats, still clutching the last of the leaflets.

Anders's parents are caught in a treadmill, constantly reminded of each other's failures and affected by them. His mother is stuck fast in her continual acts of self-sacrifice. His father feels as if he were a diving-bell, just sinking and sinking. But the glass of the bell is thick, being made of twenty years of hard liquor. From inside he observes the world and sees his son and wife. But Anders has strength enough to resist both his mother's heroism and his father's escapism and forge his own alternative.

* * *

More dramatic events lead young Kjell to awareness in *Ådalen 31*. Here too, Widerberg is trying to get back to the roots of present-day Swedish society. But here it is the true revolutionaries who are given leave to speak, those who have seen their ideas and ideals betrayed in favour of the politics of compromise.

Ådalen 31 is based on the tragedy which occurred in a small manufacturing township in Norrland on May 14, 1931, when five workers were shot dead during the course of a demonstration. The sawmill workers had been on strike for months. The demonstration was held after the conservative authorities had brought the already critical situation to a head by calling in strikebreakers. The demonstration was a manifestition of solidarity, and demands were raised for better living conditions. Nearly three thousand people walked the three mile route.

In *Ådalen 31*, too, the conflict is centered on one family, Harald Andersson and his wife and children, but the portrayal of their home life is brighter and more optimistic than in *Raven's End*. A vital driving-force in both man and wife is the sense of joy they derive from their work. They find security in the community — both an inner, at home, and an outer, that of their workmates and their families who share the same life and conditions as themselves. The threat from without (from above) is stronger and more manifest here. The village is clearly divided between a privileged class (exemplified by the works manager and his family) and the workers, in contrast to the more amorphous population structure of the urban environment in which *Raven's End* is set.

Kjell is the point of contact between the two antagonistic camps. He associates with the manager's family. The lady of the house wishes to impart culture to this intelligent and sensitive working class youth. She instructs him in music and art. She teaches him to pronounce Renoir's name with the correct French accent.

Kjell falls in love with the daughter in the family, Anne. But when her mother finds out that she is pregnant her benevolence towards the visitor vanishes. An alliance across the class barrier is unthinkable. She takes her daughter to Stockholm for an "examination," a pretext to trick her into having an abortion, which is duly performed.

The romantic love story between Kjell and Anne is one of the elements of the film for which Widerberg has been criticised by more orthodox Marxist critics. Many of them found that Widerberg had too heavily idyllised and personalised the conflicts which form the heart of the drama, thus luring the audience away from the central political argument about the class struggle.

But Widerberg's method, that of singling out a number of private destinies, also encourages and reinforces identification, understanding and empathy. What Widerberg seeks to convey with the love between Kjell and Anne — to cite a Swedish critic — is in fact a dream of union in another society. The sense of solidarity is as strong here as in Raven's End. Kjell learns to play Chopin and *Für Elise* up at the manager's house; but then goes off to practise the "Internationale" and other revolutionary songs with the working men's band in the People's House.

The idyll is the cruelly ironic frame of the subsequent bloody events. It is May, and the Norrland village is in full bloom. Kjell's mother is spring-cleaning the house. Even when her husband is off to demonstrate he must put on a clean shirt. He is one of those who fall victim to the bullets. "We can't afford to mourn," says Kjell as his mother stands in apathy staring at the body. He tears up his father's shirt and together with his brothers starts cleaning the dusty window-panes. His mother is jerked out of her sorrow and paralysis, tears off a duster and takes her place side by side with Kjell. Work becomes a symbolic rite, but it has a liberating effect.

By his choice of situations and characters Widerberg tries to make the drama tangible and comprehensible yet at the same time depict it with all its complications. He shows the father in an argument with a more class-conscious young Communist, who accuses him of reformism and softness. "It's too late for talking. The workers must act!" Widerberg also individualises the strike-breakers and their conflict. After they have been thrown out of the factory and roughed up by the angry workers, he has one of them take refuge at the Anderssons' house where they take care of him and patch him up.

The film is not historically correct on every point. Widerberg elaborates freely on the political material; in the detailed fresco that Ådalen 31 is, he seeks to evoke moods which will induce in the audience an emotional commitment. The emotions are not intended to supplant a political viewpoint but to reinforce it. This emotional technique illuminates individual lives and makes the viewer a participant in them: in Kjell's struggle, his father's, and that of the rest of the workers in Ådalen — including the strike-breakers, who also belong to those exploited and manipulated by the ruling class. But the manager's family does not merit

such understanding. They are allowed to put forward their views but their lies etched in blood can never meet with forgiveness.

Ådalen 31 is one of Widerberg's most skilfully structured films. Like Raven's End it combines the lyrical and musical creation of mood with documentary ambitions. The portrayal of the setting is powerful, meticulous and founded on intimacy. In Raven's End there is the desolate backyard, the brick housefronts, the harried greenery through which the light filters into the impeccably furnished flat. There, too, are the visitors from real life which Widerberg films in order to intensify and deepen the impression of reality. The old man sawing down the family tree in the yard. The old woman in the window dancing and singing a popular waltz. The father's drinking pals. The voyeuristic shots of Anders and his friend necking with a couple of girls in the bower. The gloom-laden account of the funeral of Kjell-Åke, the boy who dies of peritonitis because his parents could not afford to call a doctor.

The same vivid picture of reality is conveyed in Ådalen 31. The rooms of the Anderssons' home, redolent of cleanliness and openness. The blossoming countryside, where the children play and the love story of Kjell and Anne unfolds, and where the soldiers will later take up their positions behind the flowers and bushes. There are the children playing at pilots from the barn-roof. The idle youths who have lured a drunken worker into a tunnel-like fishing net after a bottle of schnaps. And then the horribly compact account of the long demonstration with its appalling conclusion. In an agitated and nervy montage Widerberg picks out those details which intensify the experience. The shock, Kjell's fury and despair, the dumbfounded soldiers, the white sheet which is laid over the dead girl and stained red by her blood. It is a scene with a strong physical impact which assumes a symbolic significance but goes on living and disturbing.

There is also a certain ambivalence about Widerberg's sensualist depiction of reality, which becomes more obvious in a film where the surface steals more of the interest from the content, such as *Joe Hill.* In this film Widerberg attempts to repeat the artistic devices used in *Ådalen 31,* and the repetition is all too evident. *Joe Hill* becomes romanticised because of the romantic shots in which he appears.

The portrayal of reality in *Raven's End* and *Ådalen 31* is complex, and both films express the kind of truth that consists of fidelity to an experience. Bo Widerberg has let the daylight in on neglected Swedish provinces and people. He has given them images reflecting their reality as well as their dreams. The music in Widerberg's films is a song to freedom. The light in his images summons forth the good and the creative in man.

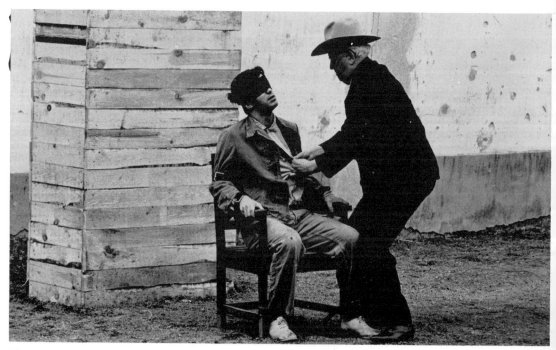

Thommy Berggren in JOE HILL

3 Undress People and They're All Alike

Vilgot Sjöman once declared: "Art is born at the frontiers of taboo." And his films are, in fact, a series of challenges. In film after film he has sought to break down frontiers. They show a striving for liberation, either internal or external. They challenge puritanism in human relations, whether social or emotional. They challenge the purism that imposes the demands of convention on our vision and on the world as a secure and harmonious entity, bound by generally accepted norms and laws.

Sjöman's *oeuvre* bears witness to a long and painful transformation, a process of self-examination and developing maturity. His triumphs have not been won without a struggle. There is still a puritan and a purist concealed beneath the dashing disguise of the rebel. But the part of Vilgot Sjöman that is still ankle-deep in the tepid mire of the traditional bourgeois conception of thought and art allows itself, with naïve enthusiasm, to be seduced by its more outspoken and exhibitionist *alter ego.*

Sjöman's route to the long-desired liberation afforded by film-making was characterised by patience and hesitation. His schools were many before he dared to take the first step. At the outset his ambitions were modest, but after achieving his first goal — his lower-school certificate — he was persuaded to join a film study-circle and it was then, he has related, that his hunger for knowledge and thirst for culture were first aroused in earnest.

He continued his studies, and in his high-school drama society he met his first and most important mentor, Ingmar Bergman. Bergman was producing "A Midsummer Night's Dream," and Sjöman was playing one of the parts.

Then Sjöman began to write himself, plays and theatrical criticism and eventually novels. His first novel, "The Lecturer," was filmed, and once again Bergman stepped in as advisor when the young author had to write his first film script. At the age of twenty-seven Sjöman learnt to dance. The first film he directed himself, *The Mistress,* was made when he was thirty-seven. Again Bergman was present as an invisible mentor. Bergman accepted the responsibility of producing the film. As a sort of apprenticeship Sjöman had spent the previous year following the shooting of *Winter Light,* documenting Bergman's methods of work in a series of television programmes and a production diary.

* * *

It may be said, then, that Sjöman embarked on his film career after mature consideration. His film *début* was an unusually accomplished work for a novice, a formally irreproachable and sensitively scripted chamber-play for three characters. *The Mistress* recounts a simple, almost banal situation, but Sjöman skillfully balances his story between general experiences and inner perceptions. The film scrutinises with equal familiarity the physical processes and the reflective ones, the skin and the nerve-paths. The language is purified and pared down, creating a framework of tangibility and intimacy.

The Mistress describes a young woman reaching maturity, her progress towards awareness and self-fulfilment. The plot is strongly concentrated in time. It is a record of four days, but between our first meeting with the woman until the film takes leave of her lies a period of roughly six months. Sjöman has chosen to relieve his story of all external drama. Instead it is present as a spiritual process.

The days that are described to us are days full of importance. But all the turbulent events and emotional conflicts contained in the story take place while the camera is absent. In this way the woman's situation is made more suggestive for us. We are made to participate to a greater extent, for we are all able to sit through the film and fill in the gaps with our own experiences and thoughts. The transitions between the four episodes of the film are abrupt, compelling us to compose the woman's drama ourselves in order to understand and accept her acts and decisions. In this way Sjöman charges his plot with tremendous emotional force. The entire experience of the public, with all the personal incidents, impressions, prejudices and understanding of which it consists, is brought into play to decide for or against the heroine.

The Mistress has only three parts: the woman, a young man and an older man. They have no names in the film; this, too, is a way for Sjöman to indicate the universality of their drama, its relevance for us who are invited to participate in it. Their everyday life is banal and easily identifiable; they are plucked out of this life, given characters and allowed to explain themselves.

Bibi Andersson in THE MISTRESS

The film opens with images of Stockholm. The young man is giving the woman a lift to work. She has taken a temporary job as a hostess at a congress. While presenting the programme in a lecture-hall she is taken unawares by a man who starts aggressively rebuking her because some important material which was supposed to have been copied in time for his lecture has not yet been delivered. The woman is speechless in the face of this violent outbreak. She is probably not responsible for the mistake but the man refuses to be pacified. He appears to be a neurotic, authoritarian person, who seems to regard the people in his vicinity solely as objects for his personal use. During the lunch break the woman goes back to her boyfriend's place. He is studying for his exams but has hurried home between lectures to cook a meal. He is obliging almost to the point of self-effacement, which is due as much to insecurity as to unconscious demands. With his devoted and deferential ways he is trying to turn himself into a part of the woman's life, but she regards with irritation the false dependence he is creating by his attitude. He gives her a table-cloth he has received from his mother. He promises to make her a bedside table, chattering away, blissfully preoccupied with himself, but at the same time letting the woman know that despite the pressure of exams he has hurried home to prepare this (rather meagre) repast. When she guiltily reproaches him, saying that she cannot accept his gifts and sacrifices, he instantly replies, "It's quite all right — I was going to eat anyway!" He is totally unaware of the way he contradicts himself all the time in his attitudes and gestures and undermines any trust that may exist between them with his wordy exertions.

From this everyday situation Sjöman builds up a very perceptive analysis of a relationship. He shows how it is handicapped by the discrepancy between the two lovers' degrees of maturity.

The woman says that she is not hungry. She stretches out on the sofa to rest. When the man kneels beside her and starts to caress her body, she pulls away. His hesitation is instantaneous. He apologises for his clumsiness. He always does everything wrong. . . Again he is thrusting responsibility on to the woman.

On returning to work, the woman meets the blustering lecturer once again. He apologises for his unjustified outburst. She accepts his explanation, and it looks as though they are about to establish some sort of *rapport.*

At this point Sjöman cuts, deliberately driving the action forward. The presentation of the three main characters is complete, and despite the trivial nature of their encounters we have received a very clear picture of them. We are already acquainted with them.

In the next scene it is early morning. The woman has just woken up from a nightmare. She lights the lamp, and from the bedside table — which is graced by a photo of the young man — she takes a letter. Suddenly the telephone rings. It is her lover. She confesses lovingly how much she is longing for him, and there is nothing in the conversation to indicate that the person at the other end is anyone else but the young man until she says: "Can't your wife hear you now?" We are immediately obliged to correct our initial assumption and apply our imagination to the events and changes that have occurred between this scene and the previous one, which was presumably several months ago. The dramatic structure which Sjöman has given the film is a very effective and suggestive one.

The following episode depicts a day of waiting. The man says that he has contrived to obtain a day off. The woman also takes a day off from work. It will be the first time they have been able to spend the entire day together.

The woman eagerly awaits her lover's arrival. She tidies up, changes her clothes and potters about in the flat. When he rings again it is to say that he will be late. He has to take his son to the dentist's. By the time evening comes there have been a great many phone-calls and delays. The woman falls asleep on the bed fully dressed. When the man eventually turns up he is harassed and shame-faced.

WOMAN: How long have you got?

MAN: Don't ask me.

WOMAN: Yes, I want to know.

MAN: Half an hour.

WOMAN: Is that all?

MAN: Well, actually twenty minutes.

WOMAN: Twenty minutes. My marriage to you!

MAN: I only make you suffer.

WOMAN: Sometimes you make me happy. . . Who cares what you make me. *They embrace desperately. Afterwards he is full of remorse.*

MAN: We can't go on like this. No more days like this. You can't stand it.

WOMAN: Yes I can.

MAN: There's so little you know, still. About yourself.

WOMAN: Am I a bad lover?

MAN: You silly thing.

WOMAN: Was he a good boy at the dentist's, your little boy?

The balance between the emotional and the rational is typical of the film and its female lead. In this sequence, the heart of the film, Bibi Andersson controls the set with admirable assurance. Her portrait evinces tremendous emotional strength and psychological perspicacity. The role is firmly grounded in a knowledge of life, and her sensitive feel for nuances enhances our understanding and sympathy for the action of the film character. Sjöman, too, shows his strength in his absolute reliance on his actress's powers of expression. *The Mistress* is an unusual and accomplished portrait of a woman.

The Mistress also signified a new attitude towards women in the Swedish cinema. Woman is presented as independent, capable of taking decisions and responsibility, as a human being attending as honestly to her emotional needs and drives as to her spiritual ones.

The remainder of *The Mistress* describes the woman's breaking free — from the two men and from the aimless existence in which she has long been trapped. In the last sequence of the film she has made up her mind. She is going to leave Sweden for a while to work and live in Rome, to give herself time for reflection. She is also strong enough to remain faithful to her emotions, her friendship with the young man and her love for her lover. But she will never relapse into the demanding ties which both of them require in their different ways. On the ferry to Germany she sends a telegram stating laconically: "Not coming back." This is the end of the story.

* * *

Sjöman's films present a series of beautifully subtle portraits of women; in most cases the director sides with the leading female characters and their struggle for a better life of their own. Women have always been more exposed to the proscriptions and judgements of society. And in his accounts of female liberation Sjöman has seen a chance to criticise existing society and challenge its conventions and dogmas.

Sjöman's women are often going through a time of crisis and turmoil, either internal or external. In *The Dress* he juxtaposes the mother approaching the change of life and her neurotic adolescent daughter. The women in *My Sister, My Love, I Am Curious* and *A Handful of Love* live in periods of upheaval and changing values. *My Sister, My Love* is set in 1782, a time when the ideas of the Enlightenment have broken through and the revolutionary forces are gathering strength in France prior to spreading throughout Europe. *I Am Curious* is an examination of the members of a society characterised by new moral attitudes and a freshly roused awareness of the political power structure on a universal scale. *A Handful of Love* is set against the background of the Swedish General Strike of 1909, with the conflict between industrial capitalism and early social democracy.

The three women in these films, Charlotte in *My Sister, My Love*, Lena in *I Am Curious* and Hjördi in *A Handful of Love*, become symbols of the subversive forces at work in society. They renounce and defy the static and the established and in their struggle to assert their own person

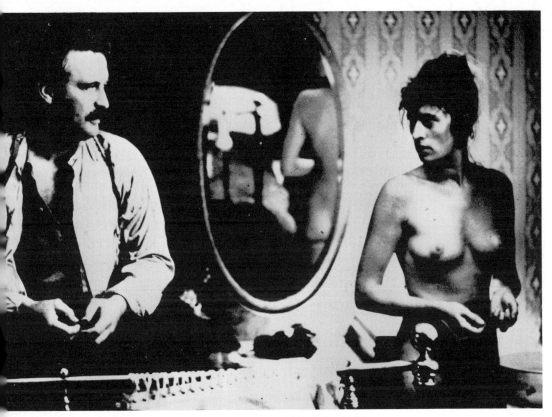

Gösta Bredefeldt and Evabritt Strandberg in A HANDFUL OF LOVE

...lities they give their loyalty to those within ...ociety who are working for change.

Both in *My Sister, My Love* and *A Handful of ...ove*, a baby is the symbol of hope for a new and ...etter life. *My Sister, My Love* is about forbidden ...ove between brother and sister. Charlotte ...ttempts to liberate herself from the conventions ...nd oppression of a male-dominated class society. ...er husband is a perfect representative of the system. He belongs to the court of Gustav III, defending his wife and the *status quo* with the same patriarchal zeal. Charlotte can only fulfil her yearning for liberation through her secret relationship with her brother. But he is not strong enough to afford her support when, wishing to complete her revolt, she tries to persuade him to flee with her, get married and live with her and the baby.

The potential consequences of the incestuous

Gunn Wållgren and Gunnar Björnstrand in THE DRESS

Gunn Wållgren and Tina Hedström in THE DRESS

love between Charlotte and her brother are indicated in an anecdote. A woman who has allegedly had sexual relations with her father is said to have given birth to a son who is an idiot. Yet after Charlotte has been shot dead in the dramatic closing minutes by a woman who is in love with her brother, the baby is delivered by a Caesarian incision and is found to be normal and healthy. The challenge of Charlotte and her brother to the rules of the lawful order triumphs.

In *A Handful of Love* Hjördis, a domestic servant, is made pregnant by her employer. The plot of the film is an intricate interweaving of love relationships, of give and take over the class barriers, in which both Hjördis and her *fiance* eventually realise that they have allowed themselves to be manipulated like helpless puppets by those who have the money and the power.

In a moment of honesty Hjördis's employer confides in her, professing ambiguously, "You must never sell yourself. At least, not in vain." Hjördis sees through the transactions they are trying to carry out with her body and her life and protests. She returns to her own *milieu* and gives birth to the baby. And when her ex-employer and lover seeks her out with new demands she dares to stand up to him. Her answer is to strike him across the face with a floorcloth. She is able to reject the blandishments of the upper class with pride, siding with her class and its forthcoming struggle. She shows the same strength, self-confidence and awareness as the woman in *The Mistress* or Charlotte in *My Sister, My Love*. It is the development of awareness, illustrated in Hjördis' struggle for liberation which gives *A Handful of Love* its moral.

In *The Dress* society is not present. Like *The Mistress* it is a chamber play for three voices: a mother, her daughter, and the mother's lover.

The *point de départ* of this triangular drama is heavily stylised. The daughter has fallen in love with a dress, an evening dress displayed in the tempting window-display of an exclusive boutique. Mother and daughter go there to shop. The daughter is firmly resolved to obtain the dress, but her mother makes various objections. She asks the saleswoman to find something more suitable for a teenager. The dress is designed for a mature woman. Her daughter, she says, lacks the necessary poise to do justice to such an expensive garment. Her mother mocks her for her clumsiness and lack of assurance.

The dress is a symbol. It represents the attainment of womanhood. The girl eventually gets her way, but ironically enough we later discover the dress in her mother's wardrobe.

As In *The Mistress,* Sjöman here gets similarly to grips with the three main characters, and in dialogue which might have been lifted straight from reality's many conversations between mothers and daughters the interplay of conflict is built up. There stands the aging woman with her censorious demands expressing unconscious hatred and jealousy of the young woman's youth and nascent adulthood. There is the daughter, with her uncertainty and her unrelieved longing. And between them, the man who is made reluctantly to assume the role of object of the two woman's rivalry, serving as a catalyst for their dissatisfaction with life.

The mother is strong and independent. She is also self-supporting, even if the antique shop she owns causes her financial worries. She does not reply to the man's wish to marry. She guards her freedom closely, though at the same time fearing loneliness. Her daughter accuses the man of passivity and weakness. "You just wait on mum!" But

the man replies with an important observation: "You'll discover that there's a bit of woman in every man and a bit of man in every woman." Vilgot Sjöman (and the script-writer Ulla Isaksson) show a sensitivity uncommon for the time in the way they construct their dialogue.

The daughter wins her mother's confidence and love by repulsing the man (after unsuccessfully trying to seduce him). With equal zeal mother and daughter seek to sweep away all traces of male dominance and conceit; an apparent family idyll, with the hallmark of a female desire to revolt, is restored for a while. But this loyalty is shortlived. In the final scenes of the film the daughter is picked up by her young boyfriend, and her mother finds herself deserted. She stands there like an exquisite antique among the choice exhibits in her shop.

As in *The Mistress,* the director's view of people and their problems in *The Dress* is distinguished by understanding and sincerity, even if the structure of the film is weighed down by excessive symbolism. (The birdcage which the mother gives her daughter should have been thrown on to the scrap-heap *en route* from the pet-shop to the studio.)

One of the finest moments in the film is the love scene between the mother and her lover. The woman sweats profusely after the love act, (apologising with "It's the transition to old age, it says so in the encyclopaedia.") The man fetches a towel. With great tenderness he tries to relieve her discomfort. He massages her, trying to soothe her anxiety and despair at this sign of aging and the erosion of beauty. Not often does one come across such a shrewd and sympathetic account of two middle-aged characters' most intimate relations.

The female portraits, in particular, are carved out with tremendous care. The role of the man in this context becomes almost inevitably more literary. Gunn Wållgren and Tina Hedström are excellent in their parts, but their empathy is occasionally disturbed by the director's conscious desire to stylise and rationalise conflicts which might have been given an even stronger personal basis and thus a greater measure of general validity.

* * *

I Am Curious—Yellow and Blue were two defiant provocations. Not only on the political and social or moral plane. The films marked two breaks with the situation of the Swedish cinema, whose foundation consisted of constructions and tales. These films broke free from navel-gazing isolation and sought involvement in the world of today. They sought to shed light on the social reality of a Sweden that had long been an area unexplored by the film camera.

The title of the films is an explicit announcement of Sjöman's ambitions, constituting a frank declaration of the director's position in the society he is attempting to depict. Sjöman did not set out to expound or prove any theories. The films are wholly non-programmatic. They describe a quest. They are an inquisitive work of research with the aim of exposing attitudes and views.

The films supply more questions than answers. Sjöman shows his *engagement* in the political and social issues which the films hold up to view, but he shows an equal lack of insight and lack of knowledge in political matters. This gives the films a certain ambivalence and hesitancy, and responses which might be expected to arise spontaneously and naturally fail to materialise. One felt this most strongly while the films were being commercially exploited. But retrospectively they serve as unique testimonies from an age characterised by self-appraisal, describing with vigour and consistency the political awakening of a generation which had too long remained passive in the face of current issues.

In the diary he kept during the shooting of the films Sjöman forestalls his critics by describing his dilemma: "For me the risk is not that I shall be prevented from saying what I want to say — but that I shall not have sufficiently piercing things to say. That my ignorance will play tricks on me."

Sjöman is curious about Swedish reality. What values, what ideas and what ideologies form the foundation of Swedish society? And he sends out a scout — the main character, Lena — to explore. With a tape-recorder slung over her shoulder and a microphone as her weapon she launches her attack (with her director as a guide and supporter), collecting facts and collating information and experiences at "Nyman's Institute." She interviews national servicemen and prisoners, tourists returning from Spain and Non-Conformists, politicians and people in power, women factory-workers and upper-class girls, and the sum total is a montage of views which is as much a truthful picture as it is a distortion.

"It is simply not possible to make political films in this tensionless society," asserts Sjöman, and therefore creates contrived tensions. Sjöman's method in these films is one of surprise and attack, and he is blatantly provocative. This applies not only to the sex scenes but to the interview sequences too. Sjöman uses the interviewees and their occasionally rather ill-considered answers for his own private ends. He does not analyse, he agitates. In the case of *I Am Curious* the people he interrogates may literally be called interview victims.

The films delineate a process of liberation on several levels. In the first place they depict an aesthetic liberation, a cinematic curiosity which is thrusting and healthy. They depict liberation in the direction of political candour and liberation in

Lena Nyman in I AM CURIOUS—BLUE

the sexual sphere. The latter is demonstrated in the film by Lena but originates from the director, and is not entirely free from exhibitionist elements.

The strength of the film is Lena's impertinent progress through a bloated Swedish society. But this progress also reveals most clearly the weaknesses of the films. Sjöman seldom allows Lena to

pause with her microphone. Her encounters with the interviewees are provocations, and there is a noticeable reluctance to engage in discussion and argument.

There are scenes in which Lena is merely agitating into thin air. She stands there, microphone in hand, addressing an imaginary target: "Do you think people stop wanting to work just

Lena Nyman and Börje Ahlstedt in I AM CURIOUS —YELLOW

where Lena provokes the recruits who are signing on to answer the question of non-violence and the refusal to perform national service. Sjöman has Lena put a question to one of the lads. Then he cuts, demanding an answer from one of the others. Sjöman is manipulating the truth by not allowing people to give their motives. He gives them no chance to reflect or to argue back.

Sjöman edits his interview material so ruthlessly that any sociological ambitions the film might have had turn out to be of dubious value. Sjöman remains loyal to the observations which he jotted down at the commencement of shooting, such as:

". . .because it is just as well to realise once and for all: You won't achieve any aesthetic refinement if you intend to tackle politics and ideas.

Make propaganda instead, crude and rude.
Right in the audience's face, if need be.
As subjectively as you can!"

But in certain scenes there is an almost mechanical trigger-happiness. In *Curious—Blue* there is an interview with a young Non-Conformist who is actually allowed to put forward his views. These are naïve at times, and he leans on his faith with grim determination. But he emerges as a human being in the immense collage of opinions which the two films comprise. Yet here, too, the spectator is deprived of the opportunity to think for himself and make up his own mind about the interviewee's ideas. The interview is immediately filed away in the subjective archives after Lena's final critical comment: "Then I got so bloody angry. . .!"

There are other interviews to which Sjöman devotes more time, for example the one with Olof Palme. But it is marked by courtesy and vagueness, not to mention a good measure of distraction. Why this sudden politeness now? Why not grill Palme in the way that Lena has been forcing her other interview victims up against the wall? After all he is better prepared to cope with this type of

because the taxes are raised? Do you think they would stop working because they aren't earning a hell of a lot of money? Don't you think their jobs mean anything to them? Are you so bloody stupid? Do you know what I think? I think you're a conservative. Oughtn't we to do something about Swedish society? Well?" What she is saying is aimed at no-one or everyone.

Sjöman often arranges his material to make it fit his purposes, and to do this he employs a dishonest interview technique. It is most marked in *Curious-Yellow,* for instance in the sequence interrogation. However, the interview with Palme is turned from a conversation about politics into a cause for complication in the story of the director and the actress. Sjöman is forestalling his critics. The interview was flat. True. But there is an explanation. In the context required by the outer framework of the film the interview has to be a failure. The tension between the director and his leading lady was so strong that the director, the interrogator, was unable to concentrate on his task.

Admittedly the objective documentary is merely a chimera, and no sociological survey can avoid being biased in some way. Sjöman wanted,

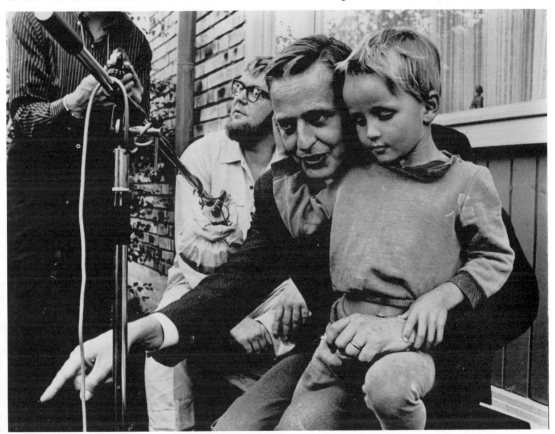

Olof Palme being interviewed in I AM CURIOUS—YELLOW

too, to avoid the lukewarm lack of involvement attaching to neutrality. But in sharpening the barbs of his *reportage* material he turns needlessly unscrupulous. Sjöman manufactures opinions, which makes it easy to understand the indignation which the films have aroused in some of their involuntary contributors.

* * *

The *I Am Curious* films sprang from a desire and a need to burst the rigid framework and plotting of the fiction film, to approach reality unconditionally and hereby create a synthesis between the feature film and the documentary. Sjöman wanted to try something new. "Something young," was his first thought. "Something with Lena Nyman," was his second. An idea was born.

Lena Nyman has a major share in the making of the film. She lends herself to others and gives herself to herself, to paraphrase Montaigne, or Godard in *Vivre sa vie.* Lena Nyman had previously worked with Sjöman in *491,* in which she played the young girl. She was also in his first stage play, "The Hatbox." Now she was a student at the State College of Drama. Despite her youth she had a good deal of experience as an actress. She had played her first major film role at the age

Peter Lindgren and Lena Nyman in I AM CURIOUS—YELLOW

of ten, having had several parts as a child actress before making *491*.

The furore about *I Am Curious—Yellow and Blue,* the provocative social reporting and the many naturalist erotic scenes all but diverted attention away from the portrait of a woman painted by the two films. The films maintain a pretence of being documentary in their description of the characters, it is true, and many people have wrongly deemed it sufficient to identify the actress Lena Nyman with the role of Lena Nyman, overlooking the gap that separates the role and the person playing that role. Neither are the director's repeated guest appearances, as Vilgot Sjöman the film director, calculated to discourage such an interpretation.

But Sjöman is also telling the story of a young woman — who happens to have the same name as the actress protraying her.

Lena may seem precocious. It is not only the information which she gathers about Swedish society that goes into her files: in her card-index she catalogues all the men she has had. There are twenty-three of them by the time she meets Börje (Börje Ahlstedt), who in the film is given the part of her lover. Her research work is therapeutic. It reveals a quest — for an identity, for a pattern. She attempts, methodically, to acquire a deeper knowledge of life, little by little converting instinct into insight.

Lena is living for the time being with her father. He is something of a Bohemian who lives off odd jobs. His past history includes the Spanish Civil War, and the film discusses the spontaneous, revolutionary radicalism of the Thirties, contrasting it with the pragmatic neutrality policies of the present day. A major part of *I Am Curious—Blue* is devoted to Lena's search for her mother, who walked out on her family when Lena was a child. Here, too, Lena attempts to fill in the contours of her weakened sense of identity.

Lena is a rebel, but a rebel with a goal. Her revolt aims at establishing an equilibrium between the emotional ties which rule her. *I Am Curious* evolves into a sad but optimistic account of lost maternal and paternal support and values yet to be attained. The methodical nature of Lena's striving becomes a means of overcoming the aimlessness which the pleasures of self-preoccupation may lead to — for she possesses this self-knowledge too.

I Am Curious—Yellow and Blue is more effective when it comes to the story of Lena than in the picture which Sjöman attempts to give of the political situation. One is caught up in the account of this young woman's road to maturity, in the description of the development of awareness which, via her attempts to gain insight into society and the problems of her environment, lead her to insight into herself.

Lena Nyman is sensationally good in this big and difficult part; cheeky, knowing and consistently in tune with the mood Sjöman wishes to create at any given moment. She enters into the part with all her soul, whether she is called on to employ her instinct for reporting, or to convey the personal conflicts in conversation with Börje or her father or her director. Lena Nyman displays an immediacy which is irrepressible, but does not exclude the possibility of self-scrutiny.

* * *

"The cinema is the medium of reactionary values," writes Sjöman in his production diary from *I Am Curious.* In his two twin films he sought to incorporate unexplored areas and win them over for an audience which had long been content with doctored myths deliberately ignoring all social tensions. Most film-makers construct their characters and destinies as if there were no such thing as the class struggle or any other clashes of interest in society. The dramatic works of the cinema are generally speaking deterministic. Ethical, moral or religious problems are debated, but the contradictions and conflicts unveiled rarely reach beyond the private sphere. Yet one need only study the challenges of Buñuel or Godard to see where a more dialectical attitude can lead. Their fearlessness *plus* their sense of responsibility have created genuinely revolutionary works.

Language is the house in which we live. By tearing down the walls we can create new rooms of air and let in new light. Formalism in its absolute form is the language of Fascism. The ceremonial, the statutory, the impenetrable. And the artist wages his struggle for liberation by denying the formalism attaching to his medium. The whole of Godard's *oeuvre* reveals a denial and erosion of conventional cinematic language. "A film is the truth twenty-four times a second," he claimed in *Le petit soldat.* Nowadays he no longer believes in this theory. In his short film *Pravda* he says that pictures lie. Only sound can convey the class struggle and the revolutionary ideas in a just manner. And Buñuel intersperses his pictures of reality with dreams, visions, shocks, continually forcing us to question the stories which pretend to be so unassailable.

In accordance with this view Sjöman's two *Curious* films remain true to his aspirations. What may be said against them is that their creator failed to consider his aims with the same lucidity.

In two of his subsequent films, *Blushing Charlie* and *Troll,* Sjöman has attempted to tackle a reality teeming with complications and contradictions by means of a more anarchistic language and plotting. This "play theory" (borrowed from Schiller) might have been Sjöman's motto for these two comedies. They seek to create a harmonious content for the lives of their characters, oases in a conformist social system which rewards discipline at work but seldom creativity. In these oases, the emotions are allowed to luxuriate like weeds, wild and chaotic. The happy bastards and the trolls may perhaps be regarded as saboteurs, but their rake's progress among those who have not yet dared to untie the knots in which society binds them is accompanied by a sense of responsibility.

Blushing Charlie is a comedy about responsibility. The main character is the lorry-driver, Charlie. He works from Monday to Friday, and at weekends he does the rounds of the bars and night-clubs with his mates, a bunch of musicians.

Charlie is satisfied with life. He lives a pretty carefree bachelor life on a barge, where he sometimes takes his girlfriend, who is a bunny at one of the clubs. Charlie's circle of friends also includes a bunch of leftwing students, who draw up blueprints for the coming revolution at serious-minded meetings, propagating the necessity of political commitment beneath portraits of Marx and Lenin and Castro. Charlie is as happy to join in their discussions as he is burning the candle at both ends with the less thoughtful musicians. But both groups regard Charlie as something of an outsider. They speak different languages. Confronted with the musicians' jargon and the political terminology Charlie seems rather naïve. Now and then the musicians gently pull Charlie's leg for being a nine-to-five worker. For the students he is something of a symbol, a guest from the working class who has to be reared to a socialist way of thinking.

A sudden unexpected lodger changes Charlie's existence. Pia, who is seven months pregnant, is homeless, and Charlie willingly helps her out. She installs herself on the barge, offering a new and more *bourgeois* alternative. She cooks, cleans, and darns his clothes, and for a while Charlie is tempted to adapt himself to the comfortable way of life she offers.

I don't know if it was Sjöman's intention to present in Pia an ironic portrait of a woman who

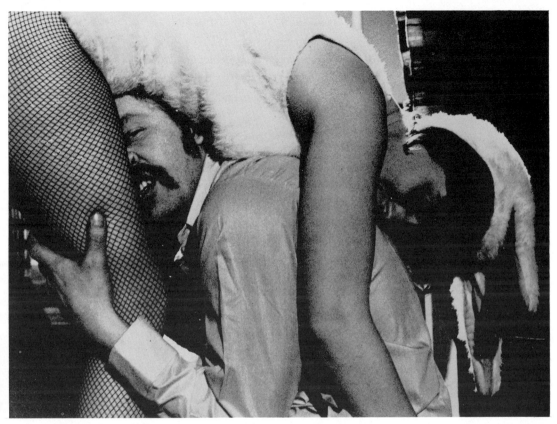

Bernt Lundquist and Lilian Johansson in BLUSHING CHARLIE

has found her place within the system. She is far removed from the women in Sjöman's other films who are working for their liberation. Like Charlie she is full of good intentions and optimism. But her wish to control her landlord's life as well as her own are irritating and suffocating in their well-meaning officiousness (Rather reminiscent, incidentally, of the young man in *The Mistress*.) Charlie is affected, if reluctantly, by her efforts, and even if he is unwilling to forfeit his freedom, he is prepared to assume responsibility for Pia and her unborn child.

Blushing Charlie is a happy film, and a film full of warmth. Charlie is played by Bernt Lundquist. Lundquist used to be in a similar line of business, and Sjöman's screenplay is largely based on the actor's own stories and experiences. This may perhaps explain the sense of intimacy which the role arouses, the directness of impact and the fidelity to a feeling which is so strong throughout the film. Charlie is the hero in a legend about humanity that is firmly rooted in reality.

Blushing Charlie almost has the quality of a fairy tale. The main character radiates an atmosphere of goodness and purity. Charlie is a knight of benevolent countenance, and at his side

in the lorry sits a long-haired child (and like the fairy-tale figure it is, we never know whether it be girl or boy). It is an incarnation of his conscience, leading him along the right path in life. These mythical figures observing and guiding people on their digressions crop up in several of Sjöman's later films. The rabbit Sture in *Troll* (who is sacrificed on the altar of love but is roused to life again shortly afterwards), for instance, or the flaxen-haired working lad in *A Handful of Love.*

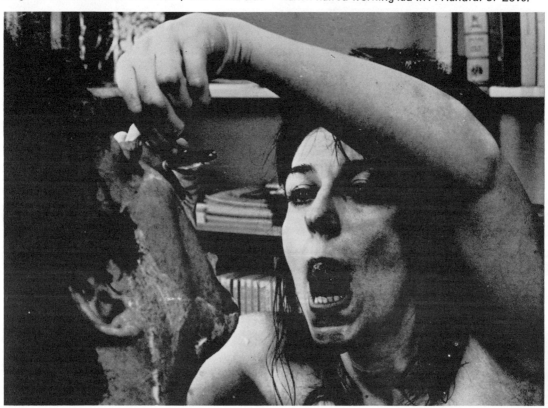

Solveig Ternström and Börje Ahlstedt in TROLL

Charlie's decisions are always for the best, and they give proof of compassion and loyalty. He agrees to help Pia. He shows up with his lorry during a demonstration for Cuba. And he throws up his job to carry out his own private revolution. In the final frames he is darting up and down the streets of Stockholm in ultra-rapid motion and into the echoing rooms of the Government Offices. He presses the visitors' button outside the Prime Minister's room and the red light on the indicator panel comes on. "Please wait." The red light illuminates the whole screen. "Socialism is yet to be achieved in Sweden" — to borrow a line from Widerberg's *Ådalen 31* — but Charlie is ready to make propaganda and influence people.

In *Troll* the situation is more acute.

The two main characters of the film have got it into their heads that screwing can kill you. It is a distressing thought, and especially for Rickard and Maja since they are in love. The mere idea is absurd, a view shared by the couple's two good friends Sture and Lillemor, who are invited one evening as guinea-pigs to prove the validity of the theory. And Sjöman uses this absurd idea to launch a well-oiled farce machinery.

Troll consists of a series of strip numbers. Rickard and Maja have a very naïve and natural attitude towards the people in their environment, whether these happen to be people in authority or old friends. Not infrequently this results in collisions, when Rickard's and Maja's spontaneous and head-on attacks are directed at bureaucracy or simply conventionally well-bred social norms.

The central part of the film describes a dinner party. Rickard and Maja have invited their friends Sture and Lillemor home, and scarcely have the initial courtesies been exchanged when the more bourgeois guests are subjected to the provocations of their hosts. Behind fixed smiles Sture and Lillemor attempt to preserve their dignity intact, although Sture is soaked to the skin after Rickard pours a glass of beer over him, and Lillemor has had

her elegant dress cut to ribbons. The guests regard this sabotage with strained composure and soon let themselves be seduced into more frivolous behaviour. The drawing-room veneer flakes off like old nail varnish. Before long Sture and Lillemor have retired into the bedroom for advanced exercises in eroticism, with Rickard and Maja peeping delightedly through the key-hole.

Sjöman has often spoken of film-making as a form of voyeurism, and the camera as a peeping Tom. *Troll* seems to be an attempt on his part to put paid to this voyeurism. And Rickard and Maja, who dare not give expression to their feelings, are his vicarious agents. *Troll* ritualises a sexual complex and makes comedy out of the need to create on the frontiers of taboo.

Troll is often very funny. The desire to have done with the prejudices and myths of love and sex is expressed with frenzied hilarity which is constantly giving rise to new slapstick scenes and a situational comedy that really comes off. The state of dissolution informing the patterns of behaviour is also demonstrated by the film language. A striving to force the pace by means of the images and the editing and so stress the absurd nature of the situations may, however, produce an irritating result. The situation is already absurd, and there is no need to underline this in the editing.

As in *Blushing Charlie,* Sjöman frequently breaks up the development of a scene with clarifying close-ups.

This sometimes arrests the experience for us.

The spectator is thrown out of the mood.

The spectator's reactions are controlled too rigidly.

And this may not have been Sjöman's intention.

But these two anarchistic yet responsible films spring from a playfulness that lures forth the emotions and liberates them. Sjöman and his actors attempt with a good deal of energy to build bridges across the schisms that exist between human beings and create a meeting-place for harmony and fellowship. Both *Blushing Charlie* and *Troll* are propaganda for vitality and *joie de vivre*.

* * *

During Lena's interview odyssee in *I Am Curious, Yellow,* one of the people from whom she demands an answer on the issue of whether Sweden is a class society replies: "Undress people and they're all alike. Put their clothes back on, and there you have a class society." This might serve Sjöman as a motto expressing his ambitions.

Sjöman undresses people to show who they really are; Lena and Börje in *I Am Curious,* Rickard and Maja and Sture and Lillemor in *Troll,* Charlie and his mates in *Blushing Charlie,* the copulating couples in *A Handful of Love* — but in these nude scenes there is no trace of narcissism, of man's love of himself.

Nakedness reveals people in all their naturalness — or conventionality. The four gentlemen introducing one another in their birthday suits by the swimming pool in *A Handful of Love* have not put aside etiquette along with their clothes. One can almost see their badges of rank tattooed on their skin.

Nudity is also sensuality and joy. Sjöman has probably never demonstrated this with a more magnificent tribute to voluptuousness than in the group sex orgy of the opera soloists in *Troll.* While performing the quartet from "Rigoletto" they indulge in pleasures which are by no means inferior to the music as regards involvement and emotional power. It is in many ways a rousing scene.

Sjöman's films come into being at the frontiers of taboo. The director challenges prejudice and prudery. By undressing the characters he could make them vulnerable, but the actors' unabashed exploitation of their bodies expresses pride and joy. The actors, "who live in a conflict between exhibitionism and *bourgeois* standards," suppress their shyness in order to combat our fear. Sjöman's nude and erotic scenes are free of all sensationalism, and here he has found a meeting-place.

Nakedness comes to be a way of getting to know people intimately — without their various disguises.

Per Oscarsson and Bibi Andersson in MY SISTER MY LOVE

4 Catcher in the Rye

For dusk and dawn
are ultimately but different sides
of this truth: that we survive
only thanks to a chance
which we never understand
or thanks to a grace
for which we know not whom to thank.
And by their alternation, by their return
they constantly confirm
sky-high above all houses and our base
calculations — that always everywhere
even for the most unworthy
for all
even for the most down-trodden
there is a living-merciful
fast point for our trust.

Day is not sheer light that dazzles.
Night is not darkness without a frontier.

Ragnar Thoursie

One could try to express what a joy it is to be alive. One could try to express what a torment it is to be alive. One could try to express what courage it requires to live: courage to be oneself and courage to be a part of others.

One could, like Kjell Grede for instance, try to create possibilities for expressing these feelings and imprinting this insight on film. This he has done in *Harry Munter* and *Klara Lust.* They are both allegories about compassion for humanity. They tell of turmoil and quiet revolt in middle-class cages in which welfare and comfort have submersed the caged people in indifference and complacency. Both of the films seek to express an enhanced sense of living. They are marked by the poet's striving for the exact and the exalted. They are dreams which express a yearning.

Grede seems to have captured and coloured his images and his characters from the inner reaches of a feeling. Then he has provided them with such a rich set of realistic characteristics that at any moment they may be super-imposed and fused with the everyday life that exists at the side of this landscape of feeling. Poetry and documentation are united. The simplicity and straightforwardness of the images, the sparseness of word and gesture, are as much an expression of truthfulness as of stylisation.

Grede's films are private ones. His stories do not lay claim to universal validity. They describe a kind of growth and maturity of feeling, and the experiences which the films gather during the course of the narrative supply the films with their own moral. *Harry Munter* describes a road towards deliverance and freedom, and the film fascinates by its complexity. In *Klara Lust* one senses repetition and deadlock; the *engagement* has turned into *pathétique.* Here people and events have become more symbolic than realistic, more haphazard and therefore more dispensable.

Both *Harry Munter* and *Klara Lust* reflect an existentialist view of life. Harry Munter, and Helge in *Klara Lust,* have both imposed on their lives the demand that they should make reality of what they themselves regard as truth. Unconcerned about their own well-being, uninterested by the attempts of their surroundings to recall them to society's conventional patterns of conduct and neurotic expectations of success, they seek to give content and meaning to their lives. They are the defenders of freedom against mediocrity's narrow-minded nexus of norms. But freedom creates alienation, an outsider feeling. It is this outsider feeling that drives Harry and Helge to try to regain an ingenuousness and an honesty that harmonise with the demands they make of themselves. Alienation is a road to liberation, but it entails an

Jan Nielsen (right) in HARRY MUNTER

equal amount of agony. For Harry the dilemma is so strong that he feels suicide to be a possibility and a solution. Both in *Harry Munter* and in *Klara Lust* there is a straightforwardness and immediacy which soothes, lending the main characters purity and innocence. Harry Munter's behaviour, his way of approaching his fellow-men, is entirely devoid of all the conventional elements of hesitation and premeditation which in most cases thwart all spontaneous attempts at making contact. Harry expresses himself directly — in words and in action. Helge considers the things around him just as real as human needs. He gives away all his holiday money — because it feels like the right thing to do. From this instinctive gesture the film derives strength and import.

Harry and Helge rarely express themselves by means of language. It is considered treacherous

Lars Brännström and Conny Larsson (left) in KLARA LUST

and imperfect and can do no more than bestow vague conditions for the fulfilment of their ambitions. They both resist the demands made of them, chiefly by their parents. Harry simply states calmly that "there are so many others too," when his parents come out with their self-seeking reproaches. Helge counters the scepticism of his mother and father by saying that he "likes feelings." Instead, they show their loyalty to the people around them by their actions, which are frequently irresolute and inadequate. But they are performed without doubt or hesitation.

It is here, particularly, that Grede lays the foundation of their alienation. He refuses to let Harry and Helge motivate themselves or to make themselves or their motives comprehensible. He locates them outside, in a silent and unknown solitude. Language cannot establish any relationship between the characters of the films. Instead Grede tries to create a link between his two heroes and the audience. A sort of conspiracy is created, inviting us to partake of the lives of these characters on a deeper level. We are given the problems of Harry and Helge as a sort of dedication. Therefore both *Harry Munter* and *Klara Lust* leave room for many different interpretations. The openness of the films amounts to a demand and a challenge.

* * *

Harry Munter is described as an over-talented seventeen-year-old. In fact the representative of the American concern which wants to buy his invention and personal services calls him "a genius" pure and simple. When the film opens he is living with his parents in the country. They expect great things of their son. They see in him the opportunity of a new life, a life in financial security as offered by the American company. His father will be able to throw up his dreary job. His mother starts an affair with the American director.

But Harry is not prepared to make the break. He feels more strongly about his responsibility towards a few lonely people round about him, whom he has befriended. Finally he accepts the offer for his parents' sake — only to change his mind again. He disappears after the plane to America has landed at Copenhagen airport, and they are all obliged to return to Stockholm. After a desperate, ritual attempt to re-unite his parents (he ties them together by their arms and legs while asleep, according to a complicated diagram), Harry takes an overdose of sleeping-pills. In an exalted vision he imagines all of the characters of the film together in a light, optimistic union around the summer house. In a smiling, affirmative round-dance they all clasp one another's hands. But Harry Munter is aroused to life once more. The dream must give way to reality.

In a sub-title to the film Kjell Grede asks the question "When does Harry Munter die?" What does the director mean by this? Several interpreters have chosen to see Harry as a Christ-figure, and there is much to support such an interpretation. Harry is presented as one of the elect. He defies death (by lying down beneath the approaching train) and the devil (the American agent). He heals the sick and tries to alleviate their pain. In one scene we even see Harry walk on the water. He comes wandering over the mist-enveloped bog on stilts. He dies and is "stigmatised" by a little boy who pricks his lifeless body with a ski-stick. He rises from the dead and in the closing frames he walks off on his father's right-hand side. Even the final vision, in which Harry gradually emerges as a sort of unifying figure of light evokes a feeling of Christian fellowship which might lend weight to this type of interpretation.

Yet it is nearer the mark to see this dream as expressing a concept of reconciliation which need not necessarily have Christian connotations. The

The walking on the water scene in HARRY MUNTER

ascetic and contemplative features of the film sooner call to mind a philosophy of Zen Buddhist type. Harry's acts of sacrifice assume an almost mystical aspect. They may be seen as purgative procedures conveying life-values. Harry Munter does not die. He is the representative of positivism — a lodestone for our trust.

Grede also tries to root his images and visions in everyday life, which is perceptively documented and rich in detail. In a similar way, Harry calculates and puts things to the test. When he lies down between the rails to await the train he has prepared his challenge and made all the necessary calculations. "It's 37 cm up to the brake-boom. And then it is 38 cm up to the cow-catcher. And it's 39 cm up to the drainage plug in the cardan axle. So it should be possible to lie underneath the train as long as you know what position to lie in. And if you dare."

Harry may be a romantic and an adventurer, but his way of approaching the world around him is based on conscious or unconscious considerations. He is always analysing, placing himself on the outside, standing back at a distance. This is most clearly depicted in a scene in the beginning of the film when he is observing his parents' bodies through binoculars as they lie exposed in deckchairs in the garden. He boldly regards the drops of sweat on his father's face, his mother's wrinkles and developing rolls of fat, while keeping at a safe distance from the scene.

The emotions afflicting the tormented people whom Harry befriends are also real. Harry never really believes that the anguished Finnish girl's paranoia has a rational basis. He tries to comfort her but denies her feeling. But the object of her dread materialises. One day her persecutor is there, and Harry masochistically lets the intruder beat him up.

Harry maintains a rational, intellectual distance to his surroundings, but there is a coldness about this which his almost overpowering capacity for human sympathy is unable to hide. Apart from the outsiders who are dependent on him — and through whom Harry also derives an importance — there are two girls, more natural and ordinary objects for a teenager's thoughts and affections. One of the girls is the typical teenage infatuation. As for the other girl, Harry sees her and sleeps with her on the side — quite unconcerned that she might feel exploited. When they are on the way out to the summer house Harry is too preoccupied with his missions of mercy either to see or to hear the girl properly:

HARRY: On Sunday he showed me the jersey. He was in the Sweden B-team once and played against Finland in Helsingborg. They lost 1-0, I think. It was a long time ago.

He's even kept the match ball, too.

GIRL: Why are you always going on about him?

HARRY: It's important for me to care about him.

GIRL: Why?

HARRY: Because I know him. Well, he's a bit boring, of course. But if you gave him up, I mean if you couldn't care less about Manne even though you know him, how could you care about the Indians or people in Burma or. . .

GIRL: Stop talking about him. I feel ill on buses.

HARRY: Well, then we dribbled a bit. His nose started bleeding again. But somehow he was happier anyway.

GIRL: Can't you hold my hand?

HARRY: Maybe I can do something for Manne. I sat there and we talked for three or four hours.

GIRL: Do you like me?

HARRY: Hmm.

GIRL: Do we have to come out here every time?

HARRY: Yes, we do. I think it's nice out here.

GIRL: This is nice too, isn't it? And this is nice. You only want me to sleep with, don't you?

HARRY: Yes.

GIRL: What if I'm in love with you then?

Somewhere *Harry Munter* is also a perfectly ordinary — if very poetic — teenage portrait of a youth who is sensitive and precocious in various ways, with a considerable lack of experience in his luggage. The film describes on a number of levels Harry's conflict-laden situation. He is a youth trying to be more mature than he is and to arrive at more adult decisions. He is the much admired near-adult for the children who eagerly allow him to lead them off on his expeditions in the introduction to the film. He makes himself responsible for the lives of Manne and the Finnish girl. He befriends his grandmother and subsequently her friend — which does not stop him begging money from them with a childish lack of responsibility (then giving it to Manne). And in the background, that continual source of conflict, his parents, with their demands and their admiration, their reliance and their helplessness.

Harry's surroundings, too, are marked by lack of definition and incompleteness. There is grandmother's house which needs repairing. There is the ravaged suburban *milieu*, where the concrete blocks of flats have not yet settled down into the still unrestored countryside. Harry stands at the intersection between memory and future.

Grede illuminates these *milieux* and people in images that have an immediate expressiveness. They have a strong poetic shimmer, a pure, crystallised beauty. Characters and objects succumb to a caressing touch in this light between dawn and dusk. They are embraced by a sensuous affection; while at intervals the darkness of uncertainty looms up menacingly, providing a fertile ground for despair.

The structure of the film, too, is poetic. The scenes merge into each other like rhyming words. The pictures, the visions, are often new, daring and staggering, but they are not offered to us in a provocative manner. They are in perfect balance with the surrounding ones. Often scenes have neither beginning nor end. The camera is mostly stationary. The images become paintings interpreting segments of a condition, an emotional experience.

Harry Munter — like *Klara Lust* — was made without a script. Instead the "plot" of the film was drawn on large sheets of drawing paper, only odd snatches of dialogue being allowed to intrude into the sketched-out situations. Parts of these "scripts" are included in the credits of the two films.

Consequently the characters, too, existed originally only as sketches. This is why Grede chose to work with actors with a strong physical presence and resemblance to the role. Grede seeks and elicits from these actors qualities which

subsequently go to make up the basis of the characterisation of each part. It may be significant that he gave the two parts which express the greatest helplessness and desperation to two comedians and farce actors: Carl-Gustav Lindstedt as the father, and George Adelly as Manne, the old man tortured by terror of death. There is an aura of sadness and faith about these two which makes Harry's involvement with them understandable.

The other parts are also filled with great sensitivity. Gun Jönsson couples a trustworthy yet firm motherliness with a flirtatious lust for adventure in her portrait of the mother. And Elina Salo as the lonely and neurotic Finnish woman is very gripping indeed. She is a funny, gentle *commedia dell'arte* figure with a despair in her eyes that is thoroughly genuine. There are few actresses who could break off in the middle of an everyday conversation and start quoting a Yeats poem, as she does in the film, with the same naturalness and total lack of sophistication.

And Jan Nielsen as Harry Munter contributes a seriousness and decisiveness which feel just as convincing.

* * *

Helge in *Klara Lust* is no more of a saint than Harry, even though his name might evoke such associations (Swedish *helgon* = saint). He has also got stuck in a conflict situation which he wishes to escape from. He is tied down to considerations and duties, to claims which he feels to be false. Partly to his mother who clings to him and in her fear of being abandoned is only swept further away from him. Partly to his young female lodger who hopes, perhaps, to share more with him than just his flat. Her little son persists in calling him Daddy, despite his repeated protests.

The dinner sequence from KLARA LUST

One day chance gives Helge an opportunity to break away from this life weighed down by the claims of others. The impulse to give away all his holiday money to a workmate who is temporarily hard up becomes for him an unconscious act enabling him to opt out of the responsibilities which he is no longer able to bear. And when he is suddenly confronted with Klara Lust, this nymph-like apparition in a black mourning-veil, his longing takes shape and is given a goal. Helge embarks on his flight towards this enchantress and a life of his own.

There is a stronger leaning towards rationalisation and the fairy tale in *Klara Lust* than in *Harry Munter.* Like the knight in the tale, Harry mounts his bicycle in order to search for his princess, even though he has neither her lost shoe nor her shoe-size with which to identify her. He is accompanied (or pursued) on his journey by his mother and "girl-friend" and her son. They cannot threaten his liberation, but neither can they refrain from trying.

Chapter two. He is in the small town where ara Lust lives. Just like that. In this film there is need for a map or compass to guide the plot to e goal, for emotion is in control. It is not simply piece of cynicism to maintain that Grede makes unusually simple for himself and his hero.

It turns out that Klara's surname is Larsson and at she is the daughter of the most influential an in these parts. A stone's throw from his xury villa is a condemned house inhabited by a thetic bunch of down-and-outs. There is the ise Fool, who quotes Mayakovsky and tends his scible, sick father. There is the Murderer, who allenges Helge with a knife at the dinner table. here is the Blind Man whose longing it is to fall ver and hurt himself without anyone helping him. here is the Kiosk Manageress waging her fruitless ttle against the authorities. And there is the lcoholic, the Cripple and the Lover, who also ves Klara Lust. They now turn to Helge for help. r is it the other way round?

Helge — like Harry Munter — wishes to don the artyr's cape of kindness, but his exercises in umanity lead nowhere — except, of course, for inging him nearer his adored Klara Lust. And ere is probably nothing that mankind can more sily do without than this species of self-sacri- cing martyr. Grede loses his hero in a fog of norphous benevolence. Helge's honesty and timism become meaningless phrases; if he anages to win the blonde enchantress into the argain they certainly won't live happily ever ter!

Klara Lust does little to develop the humanistic essage which Harry Munter sought to put across. rede creates a dangerous distance between the al inter-personal social problems which exist, and e romantic, symbolic conflicts he creates in lara Lust. The characters in the film soon turn to puppets in a game in which they listlessly rrender their lives in the face of power. The xistentialist belief which holds that every human being is responsible for himself is no longer valid, at least not for anyone else but Helge.

The *lumpenproletariat* which Grede has assembled fails to function either symbolically or realistically. And language — for which both Harry Munter and Helge harbour such mistrust — is used to alienate these rejected men and women from the audience. Neither the Mayakovsky quotations nor the other scattered sentences with which they attempt to communicate can serve as anything but soothing embellishments. ("This close correspon- dence with life itself is what is called mystique. In this sense everyone is a mystic.") They are posies of words brightening up a poor but complacent existence. Not even in the kiosk manageress's long monologue, in which she seeks to justify realis- tically her hopeless life, does the director extract anything but a sort of almost indecent sentimen- tality. This is despite the fact that the actress (Mari Isedal) puts her bitter message across with utterly genuine despair, reaching far beyond the actual words. The context is completely wrong, and Grede transforms a profoundly human confession into a sacrifice on the altar of pseudo-humanist pathos.

Klara Lust, too, is driven along by a sort of love message. Love is the cure for pain and oppression. But when Grede has confronted the characters in the film with love and grace, no liberation is offered. Freedom is an illusion. The film ends in romantic falsity when the outcasts and oppressed are dispatched to some kind of Shangri-la of brotherly love. They flee to "somewhere where it is beautiful."

It is tragic. Klara Lust shows how ambition and feeling are corrupted into nothingness. But it started off so well. In a concrete situation with real problems which more than grazed the essential issues of freedom and responsibility which the film seemed to want to discuss.

This is how it started. It is the end of the last day before the holidays. The machines in the workshop where Helge works are to shut down. The workers chat about holiday plans and destinations. One of Helge's work-mates asks him to lend him 1000 kronor, though he cannot say what he is going to use the money for. "Something bloody awful has happened!" One after the other they pack up and go. Helge stands alone at his machine. When he is reaching for a transistor radio behind a guillotine press the machine suddenly starts up. Helge cannot free his arm, and the big blade descends menacingly. Then, as inexplicably as it started, it stops, the cutting-edge a fraction of an inch above Helge's outstretched wrist. It is as if a miracle has occurred.

Helge suddenly seems to regard his environment with completely fresh eyes. It emerges in an entirely new and clear light. A glass of water on a bench. The sun shining on the wood chippings and dust. Helge touches his hand and holds it up against a jet of water. A great feeling of liberation seems to have taken hold of him. When he walks over the sunlit yard the reflection of his shadow is mirrored in a pool of water, and Helge seems to see himself for the first time. He has already given his money away. The observation of things takes on a contemplative, everyday exactitude, and the light bestows both peace and freedom.

Even in the soundtrack a new feeling of hope becomes evident. First there is the harsh, realistic din of the workshop, attempting to drown the terse comments of the men. Then there is a compact silence followed by a triumphant Mahler symphony.

There is a similar compactness about the following scenes. The interior of Helge's flat. There we see his mother anxiously laying the table for her fiftieth birthday party: "Do you think these cups are funny?" There is his lodger-girl-friend with her little son. Here the film strikes an everyday note which is thoroughly convincing in its haphazardness and confusion. And it is heightened at the encounter with his mother's coffee-drinking, gossip-ridden friends and during his father's brief visit.

Then occurs Helge's fateful meeting with Klara Lust, and gradually the realistic perspective gives way to an increasingly unhappy plunge into the obscure and the obvious.

* * *

Yet despite the faults exemplified by *Klara Lust* Kjell Grede is unique as a film-poet in Swedish cinema. This was evident from his very first film, the exquisite miniature *Hugò and Josefin,* which shares the same poetical view of reality shown in *Harry Munter* and *Klara Lust.* There are few film-makers who are able to "sensualise" the characters and objects in front of the camera in the way Grede does.

Grede has expounded his attitude to the cinema in an interview:

"What I least of all wish to make are naturalist films. What I least of all wish to make are films recording the reality we can see, I mean a sort of documentary. But I still like films like that. I enjoy watching films like that when they come on television.

"I have a strong urge never to take any interest in reality in a film except as a means of conveying a feeling. Nothing else interests me.

"I think it is important to try to depict our positive visions. I believe in the power and the strength that comes of having some kind of utopia before you, of trying to see more clearly what it is you are longing for. There I think the cinema has a wonderful function to fulfil, if it could suddenly start putting into visual terms what we really long for, what we really dream of. The cinema may go on being a dream factory, but fabricating true dreams instead of false ones. Dreams with a use."

In 1974 Grede completed his fourth feature film, *A Simple Melody*, about a young fireman who suffers from dizziness. And in the background there is another parental pair, with new obligations and new demands. . .

Below: Jan Nielsen celebrates his courage in HARRY MUNTER

Eddie Axberg and Stig Tornblöm in HERE IS YOUR LIFE

5 Let a Hundred Pictures Burn

"As soon as we express a thing we reduce its value in a curious way. We think we have dived down to incredible depths, and when we come to the surface again the water-drops on our pale finger-tips no longer resemble the sea from which they come. We think we have discovered a treasure-chamber full of miraculous riches, and when we come up into the daylight again we have only fetched up false stones and bits of broken glass; and yet the treasure continues to glow everlastingly in the dark."

Maeterlinck

Jan Troell has created the two most successful films in the history of the Swedish cinema. His films *The Emigrants* and *The New Land* have cost the most to make. They have been seen by the greatest number of people. They have made the most money. Both films have been nominated for Oscars. A world market has opened up for them and their director.

In more respects than these they are Sweden's answer to *The Sound of Music*.

It is not difficult to explain the great success that both films have achieved. They are based on, and constitute a faithful illustration of, Vilhelm Moberg's trilogy of novels "The Emigrants," "The Immigrants" and "The Pioneers," which is virtually a national monument in modern Swedish literature. The films form a romantic and pictori-ally beautiful fresco. It often has a fairy tale's tone and simplifications. It has a sentimentality and tranquillity which make it easy for the viewer to step into the picture and wander around in the harsh but colourful landscapes, slightly detached from the characters. The films seem as clean and healthy as a walk in the woods.

The Emigrants and *The New Land* describe the destinies of a handful of emigrants at the end of the Nineteenth Century. They tell the story of some farmers who take leave of their desolate patches of land in Småland and after great privation and hardship reach the promised land, America, where they try to make a better, more secure future for themselves.

The novels live by virtue of their epic weight. The human destinies — with Karl Oskar and his family in the centre — are interweaved, and the historical epoch, marked by poverty and social injustice, is brought alive in a very concrete way. Poverty and hardship strengthen the characters in their resolve to seek a different kind of life. There is very little of this aspect in Troell's film version.

Troell is a lyricist, not an epic-writer. To entrust him with a work like Moberg's is tantamount to asking a water-colour artist to paint a mural. Troell has devoted a good deal of care and time to his work, and certain details may flare up with a unique glow, but the entirety is lost in the pastel hues of a romantic haze.

In his *début* work, *Here Is Your Life*, these

lyrical qualities are effective. In fact they carry the film forward. It is also a sentimental glance back at a past epoch, but it centres naturally on its main character, young Olof, with whom both the director and the viewer are able to identify. *Here Is Your Life* is also based on a literary model, Eyvind Johnson's series of novels called "The Novel about Olof", and the film has borrowed its title from the second of the four volumes. It is an autobiographical novel, a sort of Swedish equivalent of Gorky's classic trilogy.

Here Is Your Life describes a young person's road to maturity. Even before the opening shots of the film young Olof has packed his rucksack in order to venture out into the world. He takes leave of his foster-home, with his foster-mother's quiet words of admonishment ringing in his ears long after the train on which he is travelling has left the station.

Out into the world: that means work and responsibility. Olof roams the poverty-stricken countryside of Norrland, from one job to another, driven by his wanderlust. He regards life and the conditions it offers with almost wordless acceptance. But when working as a timber-floater and at the sawmill or the forge, he watches his comrades with an ever increasing knowledge "that his life will not turn out like theirs." *Here Is Your Life* shows how Olof gains insight into the potentialities of language and the necessity of action. He grows in human and social awareness. In the end he is able to formulate his longing in more concrete terms. The final scenes of the film show a human being who has found himself and found his mission in life. In the last shot Olof is still wandering onwards, but his goal has a name and a purpose. When Troell makes the camera rise and hover high above Olof as he walks on down the line, finally taking in the magnificent Norrland countryside, he shows that Olof's world no longer

Gudrun Brost and Eddie Axberg at the start of HERE IS YOUR LIFE

knows any bounds.

Troell's best short films are portrait studies *Portrait of Åsa,* about a little three year old girl and *Johan Ekberg,* about an old-age pensioner, and these films breathe purity and immediacy, showing that Troell sees as much with his eyes as with his heart. It is the same intimacy that is present in these short poems of every-day existence which imbues the film about Olof with life.

Here Is Your Life is a retrospective look at an era, but it also functions on a personal plane as a reminder of time gone by, as memories of a lost youth. The film is nostalgic and melancholy in tone. It depicts a piece of reality re-created. It is this that gives the film its structure. The introductory episodes are short, shorn off. Only the essence of events is left. Here Troell is employing rationalisations and poetical abbreviations. The whole of the introductory sequence has the character of memory images recalled in glimpses filtered through time and the wistful feeling of something long since fled, to eventually attain their definitive form.

The introductory montage shows Troell's poetical relation to the text. Olof is followed over he razed heath by his foster-mother. The whistle of a train serves to identify the walkers' destination. The leave-taking between the two is not portrayed visually. Instead, we hear the anxious, awkward farewell of Olof's foster-mother when he is already seated on the train, where the view from the window has become one with his dreams. Troell has created a beautiful symbol of Olof's longing: a bird — blue like hope — hovering over a golden landscape. When the train journey is nearing its end the carriage with Olof in it seems to travel on into his parents' house. Outside the compartment window the family portraits glide by, and suddenly Olof's brothers and sisters are standing there. We hear the train braking. Olof is home.

ke Fridell, Ulla Sjöblom and Eddie Axberg in HERE IS YOUR LIFE

The introduction of the film is dominated by these fragmentary scenes in which dream and memory are combined. Olof is not yet really tangible. He is one of life's onlookers, someone who has not yet partaken of it. Gradually the episodes become more substantial when Olof has found his language and can express himself in the particular situation he finds himself in. He stands up to the sawmill boss, who cannot see any point in letting the machines stand idle, although an apprentice-boy has just been fatally injured by a falling timber-load. He protests against the meanness of the cinema operator and his bowing and scraping to the *bourgeoisie.* He discusses politics and life with his best friend Fredrik. But when it comes to describing Olof's political awakening the scenes practically assume the character of a mechanical *résumé.* Olof reads militant poems, studies, demonstrates. But when, as here, there is no other character to whom Olof can relate his new insights, no convincing portrayal of his development is achieved. Not until Olof is picketing and agitating for revolution with his workmates in the engine-sheds does Olof (and Troell) find himself.

Troell, who shoots and edits his films himself, tells his story chiefly in pictures. He almost seems suspicious of the possibilities of the spoken word. Troell never gives interviews. His films show what he has to say.

In *Here Is Your Life* it is a good deal, and often very prettily said too. Troell depicts the job of timber-floating as a constant journey, with death as a shadowy companion. He depicts love as a bike-ride, intangible and captivating. But we meet Troell's most beautiful vision in "the tale of mist and tuberculosis," August the timber-floater's story about his wife. It is an almost hallucinatorily beautiful sequence in colour — the rest of the film is in black-and-white — with diluted, almost transparent pictures, in which the transformation effected by the dream bestow light and peace on the frail and dying woman. August's wife crosses the golden fields to fetch water at the spring. In the pale mist she suddenly sees the souls of her dead children, happily running in the grass around her. And the children draw her down with them into the grass, luring her to rest.

With pictures Troell experiences total freedom. Pictures express the essence of emotion, and are its embodiment.

In the *Emigrant* films, too, Troell relies on the expressiveness of the pictures, but here not even a thousand well-composed *motifs* can conceal the fact that the films lack a consistent screenplay and structure. Episode is added to episode, *tableau to tableau,* with tireless zeal, but the trouble with these pictures slipping past is that they have all been allotted the same value. There is no tension between the pictures and the scenes; there are no eruptions and no rests. Simply a calm and staid statement of fact. And as a method this is dangerous in several ways. Even violence becomes an aesthetic commentary — as in the Indian attack in *The New Land.*

The films also constantly waver in their attitude to the characters they portray. Karl Oskar, his wife Kristina and his brother Robert occupy one centre of the action. We are aware of the others in the emigrant collective and their presence, but they never really take shape. Troell tries, but does not manage to interlace these human destinies in an effective way. They cross one another apparently at random — when the director needs help with filling in the story of Karl Oskar and Kristina but there is no real affinity between them. The underlying hesitancy of the film results from the dilemma whether to depict the collective as a whole or the selected family.

Karl Oskar and Kristina remain, in fact, curiously anonymous despite the length of time we spend in their company — almost seven hours altogether. They cannot formulate their thoughts, and this is, of course, one of the reasons for their vulnerability and tragic stature. They belong to the proletariat, the poor, and their yearning for a more meaningful and richer life is not hard to understand. They are unable to put their yearning into words, but it is there.

If Karl Oskar and Kristina lack a language, then Troell should be able to help. But he is bewitched by pictures. Out of the poverty, the privations, the daily misery, he creates an exquisite montage of man battling against nature, in which the pictures of the stony fields and the routine of hard work are so beautiful that their import is falsified. As a

Eddie Axberg in THE EMIGRANTS

result, Troell deprives Karl Oskar of his motive for setting out for the new country. His decision becomes a mere statement to be added to the other laconic turning-points of the film. Only in the character of Robert is the dream of a better life embodied. Robert is played by Eddie Axberg, who also played Olof in *Here Is Your Life,* and these two parts are twin souls. Curiosity and adventurousness are present in them as a real vital force. But above all it is the actor who spontaneously conveys these traits in his acting. Troell does not give him or the part any active support. Robert's decision is illustrated by a metaphor. He drops his wooden clog in a stream and allows the shoe to be swept away by the current. In the next shot Robert tells of his desire to emigrate.

What *The Emigrants* and *The New Land* most lack are fully developed scenes in which the characters can come closer to us. Troell often contents himself with hints, leaving the audience to draw the conclusions. Robert seems more alive because he is given a greater number of scenes in which to set out his motives. As for instance in his contacts with his best friend Arvid, or the English lesson with a young girl on the boat to America, or his conversation with Kristina after returning from his horrific gold-prospecting odyssey. As a rule these scenes are filmed in calm two-shot sequences, alternating in a steady editing rhythm, and, above all, the characters are allowed to have their say.

It is presumably the script that is to blame for the fact that so many episodes with strong inherent dramatic potential fall flat — such as the arrival in America, the disappearance of Lill-Märta, Fina-Kajsa's death — and that the characters glide past out of reach in the way they do.

What mars *The Emigrants* and *The New Land* is Troell's ambition to include as many episodes from the original work as possible — and this fidelity is devastating. The script should have aimed at greater density and concentration. That it is possible to depict a personal and a collective situation simultaneously, to present individual destinies in an historical context, is demonstrated by such films as John Ford's *The Grapes of Wrath* and Sydney Pollack's *They Shoot Horses, Don't They?*, films with many features in common with

Troell's epic. Another film that presents a considerably more powerful and gripping vision of the American dream is Elia Kazan's *America, America,* in which both the director and the main character know where they are heading and why.

Troell also fails with the actors. Max von Sydow's acting has never been so stilted and dumb as in *Here Is Your Life* and the *Emigrant* films. And Liv Ullmann is never given the opportunity of

THE EMIGRANTS: Liv Ullmann as Kristina

taking many steps outside her grand role as a winsome and persevering Earth Mother and really becoming a character of flesh and blood. The actors are hampered by the strange dialect they are forced to speak. Liv Ullmann, Eddie Axberg and Monica Zetterlund struggle desperately with their guttural r's, but the last two sabotage the general consistency whenever they feel like it — which is just as well. I do not know if Troell thinks he achieves greater authenticity by using this strained intonation. The effect, at any rate, is the opposite; it is a deadweight on the acting. On the other hand, notice how close Liv Ullmann comes to us in Troell's American film *Zandy's Bride.* There she is given a free hand with the part, and all her superb qualities as an actress come across. She radiates

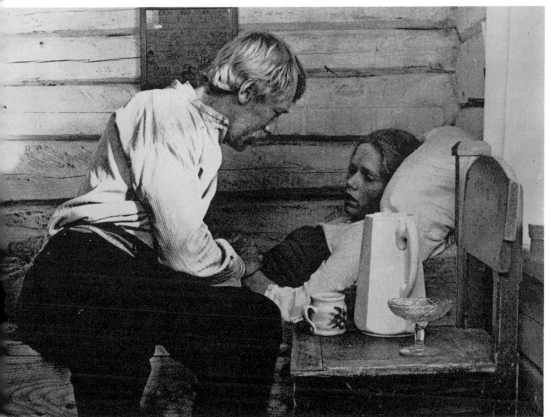

THE NEW LAND: Max von Sydow as Karl-Oskar attends his dying wife

humour, warmth, sympathy and the sort of authority of which she is deprived in her portrayal of Kristina.

Bearing in mind the glossiness of *The Emigrants* and *The New Land,* and Hollywood's adoption of Jan Troell, one might fear the worst of *Zandy's Bride.* But instead it is a firm and moving story about two lonely people who are brought together by the quirk of fate that the lonely-hearts' column constitutes. Troell takes pains to penetrate under the skin of these people, and this story, which certainly has some trite features, takes some unexpected turns.

Zandy, who in the opening scenes of the film is riding to the stage-coach depot to pick up the bride he has caught by means of a marriage ad, is another of those people with no language whom Troell adopts in his films. The introduction is imbued with gentle humour. Zandy's clumsy attempts to scrutinise the object he has ordered from a distance are soon discovered by the prospective bride, who, amused, submits to the advertiser's embarrassed advances. But Zandy's more brutal sides are soon exposed. He regards his bride as a commodity, as a necessary fixture to be added to the others on the farm. Every home must have its woman, and the family must be perpetuated. Zandy passes remarks about her age and physical attributes, issues orders and demands absolute obedience. On the first evening he rapes the woman, who has been hoping to find a deeper sense of comradeship with the man she has married before having to fulfil the obligations of the marriage contract.

Zandy's Bride is perilously close to melodrama, but Troell keeps his balance longer then expected. He is backed up by the two players, Gene Hackman and Liv Ullmann, who have seen a chance to create two plausible and interestingly contradictory characters out of the comparatively stereotype roles. Behind the taciturn domestic tyrant, Hackman exposes insecurity and anguish. He seems to be longing for a chance to express his feelings spontaneously and directly but he simply does not know how. He has no words available to help him. He is a man without a language — Troell provides this dilemma with a drastic illustration in a scene where Zandy visits his parents. Father, mother and brother eat a meal together and hardly a word is uttered. They communicate by means of gestures, and these are often most aggressive. Troell shows how the lack of language gives rise to violence.

Nor is Liv Ullmann's part cast in the same mould throughout. She does not turn into the careworn, downtrodden slave that circumstances might justify. She is practical, packing up her dreams in her spacious trunk — for the time being. She is also able to stand up to her husband's provocations by virtue of her greater experience of life. She refuses to become the victim of her own inhibitions or her husband's.

But about two-thirds of the way through, the film loses its firmness, and Hollywood *clichés,* which Troell is not quite able to control, threaten to take over. At a barbecue evening with a set almost borrowed from an old opera poster the rot sets in, and when Susan Tyrrell waltzes off into a fiery flamenco by the campfire and lures Gene Hackman up into the hayloft we are watching a talented American actress making a fool of herself. Troell now loses the two main characters, and they do not find each other until the closing scenes of the film. Then, by way of compensation, they are all the better. Not only do Zandy and his wife get through to each other in these scenes, where Liv Ullmann's acting, especially, shows powerful authority, but the film manages to get itself and its intentions under control. Here are insights that feel thoroughly genuine.

The life and dignity of the film stem from the interplay between Zandy and Hanna. The scene shots have a strong lethargic streak, as so often with Troell, and by dint of constant repetition they eventually become much too poetic and monotonous. But in the construction of the scenes between Gene Hackman and Liv Ullmann, Troell is always on a par with the action. The long medium shots and close-ups express tranquillity and closeness and immediacy. Here Troell shows what a shrewd intimist he is.

Troell does not lose his theme by premature cutting. He waits with the camera fixed on these people who are exposing themselves to us, and he waits until everything has been said — even if these people have very little to say to each other.

This is reminiscent of the best scenes in *Here Is Your Life.* Zandy's and Hanna's search for themselves does not require as many journeys as Olof's. They are pioneers — just like Karl Oskar and Kristina — but it is not primarily treasures of the earth they are searching for. They are searching for each other, the chance of reaching another human being.

With his film Troell shows that they have every chance of success.

Liv Ullmann and Gene Hackman in ZANDY'S BRIDE

Rolf Larsson and Sven-Bertil Taube in HUGS AND KISSES

6 Figures in a Landscape

"Anyone who today doubts the justification of the fiction film (literature is, of course, more frequently questioned) must regard this *genre* as an exchangeable institution (rather like the monarchy — its function could just as well be cut down and taken over by another institution or activity). The reason for continuing to make fiction films would thus be the opposite: that the film can communicate experiences and provide knowledge which are not formulated anywhere else in society, with the same significance and effect.

"For this to happen, I think that the director must take a *risk,* in the sense of accepting that he too is a part of the set-up which he intends to depict. If he wishes to criticise certain feelings, strivings or actions he must do so on the basis of his own personal experience. Only then does his criticism stand a chance of becoming effective in this particular form, i.e. expanding beyond what is purely conceptual and what we *could have imagined beforehand.* The point is, in other words, not to lapse into self-censorship in the name of any particular brand of decency and into rationalisation of one's material — this inappropriate mixture of private and public — since the socially interesting thing in this connection is that the material looks as it does in spite of everything.

"This is not a question of anti-intellectualism. Before the material can be filmed it must be distanced and visualised; if well-filmed, this too assumes documentary value. To bourgeois society also belong the dreams and the mentality it engenders; in order to criticise these dreams and this mentality one must above all be painfully familiar with them, and then put them on show — i.e. one must take the inconvenient detour via concretisation.

"This, I believe, is the concern of the fiction film and here it finds its social function. Perhaps there will always be a conflict between concretion and clarity, between sensuality and utility. Insofar as one experiences this conflict there are only two alternatives: to strive for greater clarity without abandoning one's material or to take up another occupation."

Jonas Cornell wrote this credo on the occasion of the *première* of his second feature film, *Like Night and Day.* Here, as in his *début* film, *Hugs and Kisses,* he defends and professes his faith in the rules and possibilities of the fiction film. Cornell's films *are* fiction, roles, patterns — plot-structures with visible and concealed tensions, action constructed so as to alarm and provoke reflection.

There is nothing frivolous about Cornell's utterances or his films — one should not be misled by the fact that *Hugs and Kisses* has been dressed up as a comedy. It is a serious film. Which does not prevent it from being very funny. It just means that Cornell takes a serious view of comedy.

Hugs and Kisses is based on the comedy of manners. The film might just have well have been called *La règle du jeu,* and the title would not have been the only thing linking it with Jean Renoir. There is a similar way of regarding the protagonists, with understanding and sympathy, and a reluctance to sit in judgement over their occasionally whimsical behaviour. The spectator is given the chance to take an interest in and reflect upon the decisions and motives of all the participants in equal measure. The spectator's freedom of choice is total, that of the protagonists only relative. They have their positions to defend, their places in the pattern, which they may either be consumed by or revolt against.

In the introduction to *Hugs and Kisses* we see the formation of the eternal triangle, that of husband, wife and resident friend. But Cornell is not setting the stage for the more trivial sort of conflicts. His plot is more subtle than that.

John, who may one day become a writer, has just been thrown out by his ex-girlfriend. He looks up his old class-mate Max, an extremely well-situated member of society with a directorship in his father's company. Max offers to put John up for a few days, an offer which John is not slow to accept. As they are leaving Max's office together, John automatically opens the door for his benefactor, and Max accepts the gesture as his due. John silently curses himself for his fawning, but is is obvious from the outset how the roles are to be distributed.

John moves in with Max and his wife Eva — as butler, companion and surrogate child. Max's and Eva's marriage is not as happy and harmonious as it appears — appearances are deceptive. Max and Eva sometimes talk about how happy they are, and if one simply took their words at face-value one might be deceived by their voices. But their faces reflect sorrow and regret for something that is missing. Cornell's films often function in this way; image and sound are frequently at variance. For this reason attention is required of the spectator.

Max and Eva need John as much as he needs them. He serves as a distraction from their problems. He opens the doors of their matrimonial prison, bringing them a sense of romance and adventure with his bohemian ways and his tales of voyages of exploration to foreign parts. With his vagueness and vulnerability he offers Max and Eva a chance to involve themselves in a third person, to renounce their own self-satisfaction, which is the most serious threat to their unification as human beings. John's job is to deputise as the child they have never had.

But since so much in the film is expressed in make-believe games, it is important never to reveal the real significance of the relationships for those involved. In fact Max and Eva seem to have denied the personal element for a long time, out of laziness or fear rather than lack of feeling. Jargon has come to replace conversation, gestures have come to replace a serious *rapprochement* between them. In the end they find this tormenting, especially Eva.

Hugs and Kisses discusses the serious problems of living together, but does so in comedy form. From the moment John awakes his hosts on the first morning in his new home with a neatly laid breakfast tray, the director no longer bothers about sticking too tenaciously to the realistic perspective. *Hugs and Kisses* is a comedy as graceful as it is burlesque. Thus John — in gaily patterned underpants and vest — resolutely enters Max's and Eva's bed to share their breakfast there. Pouncing on the tea and toast, John has cleared the tray almost before Max and Eva are properly awake. The three of them form a cosy little *ménage-à-trois* in bed, a play-pen of generous dimensions.

Harmony has been restored in Max's and Eva's home, but happiness is no permanent state. The rules of the game — for it is still very much a game we are witnessing, with emotions as stakes and winnings — move cautiously in accordance with the rules they have laid down themselves, if tacitly. But when one of the players suddenly makes an unexpected stray move, the two others immediately become alarmed. One day John takes home a girl, the outspoken and generally liberated Kickan. Her palace-revolutionary opinions disturb the equilibrium of the relationships. Max and Eva are agreed — Kickan must go, and they put into effect a plan to eliminate this disruptive element. The plan is for Eva to seduce John and she succeeds all too well in her intent. In the final scene the roles have been switched. Max sits outside the bedroom excluded. Purposefully he dons John's

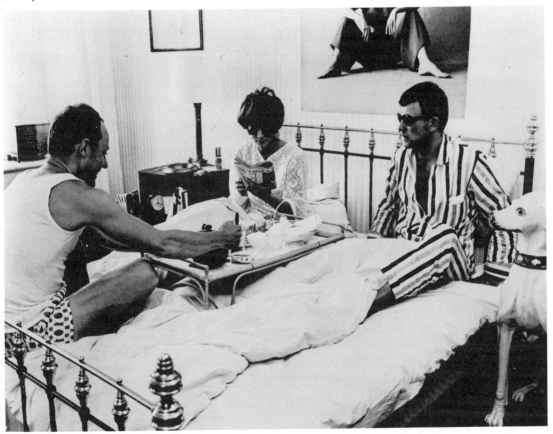

Håkan Serner, Agneta Ekmanner and Sven-Bertil Taube in HUGS AND KISSES

vest on top of his elegant jacket. The moral could be formulated à la Marivaux: "Do not trifle with love."

Hugs and Kisses is, then, a serious comedy, in which there is interplay between laughter and tears. But the smiles are shown and the tears concealed, and this contributes to the strong sense of frustration that the roles evince. In a scene at a photographic studio — Eva works as a model — Eva is waiting for Max to pick her up. She is standing and talking to Jan the photographer when he suddenly embraces her, quite spontaneously. He looks at her seriously.

JAN: Though I know what you're wishing at this moment. Really.

EVA: Nothing.

JAN: That it was Max, standing here. And that he was being nice to you.

Suddenly Max is standing in the doorway. He regards the couple standing in the middle of the large, light room. They catch sight of him and smile.

JAN: She's wishing that it was you standing here. And that you were being nice to her.

MAX: If there's one thing that I find really touching, if there's one thing that really moves me, it's two people who are really fond of each other. It's as though we had forgotten the heart in this day and age. What with all the stress and strain, all the machines, all the cars. I am touched. I am going to. . . a tear!

JAN: Well I'll be buggered!

EVA: Well, well.

MAX: You saw it, didn't you? A genuine, sorrowful tear, you can't fool me. Eva! You saw the tear, didn't you?

And Max reverently wipes away the tear that has run down his cheek, demonstrating his interpretation of the role of "the deceived husband." He is holding up a mask, like a shield or a signal.

The characters in *Hugs and Kisses* — especially Max and Eva — hide behind masks, and the elements of farce and comedy often constitute weapons for breaking down these mimic fortifications. But when demasking takes place the human being behind the mask does not reveal himself but swiftly adopts a new role, as protection and as a way of coping with the situation.

In this way *Hugs and Kisses* functions on two levels, visible and invisible. Cornell requires us to devote critical attention to what we see and hear. His scenes always have a false bottom, and the effect may be either farcically absurd or mysteriously poetic.

The farce sequences of *Hugs and Kisses* resemble Howard Hawks's comedies. Cornell employs methods similar to Hawks's to startle the audience. The bouts of farce are generally aimed at Max and Eva, who are both controlled and composed and therefore vulnerable. Irrational behaviour and actions are introduced in realistic situations — children speak and behave like adults, adults act like children, roles which are presumed to react according to a given pattern act at variance with these expectations. This irrational conduct offers a flight into irresponsibility, and both Max and Eva gratefully accept the opportunity.

In the lyrical sequences Cornell has found a tone which is wholly his own. Here, too, reality is the kernel, but it is suddenly presented to us in an unexpected light. One of the more important and most beautiful scenes occurs on the evening after John has moved into his room. He is unable to get to sleep, so Max and Eva tuck him up and give him his catskin, which he has to have between his face and the pillow if he is to sleep. While Max reads him a goodnight story, a chapter from Jules Verne's "The Mysterious Island," we see Eva go into her bedroom. Slowly she undresses in front of the full-length bedroom mirror, and exactly when Max reaches the climax of the story, the discovery of the mysterious island, we see Eva naked in front of her reflexion. She is the mysterious island; perhaps she is already appearing in the dreams of the sleeping explorer John. Max can only oblige with the description, the map-reading. Of the three he is the one who is most emotionally petrified and condemned to remain in his mould.

In an interview about *Hugs and Kisses* Jonas Cornell said: "The story, the screenplay, is very important for me. I do not set out to discover reality in my films, but go to meet reality with a pre-determined pattern. I always work with a hypothesis, as it were, and this hypothesis is the plot of the film. I do not improvise my way forward, and I do not think there is any meaning inherent in events around me. I have to create that meaning. And I try to do that by filming."

Cornell's films may be called literary. This does not in any way prevent his films from possessing a strong visual expressiveness. Cornell is certainly the most form-conscious of the younger Swedish film-makers. His films show a bond between intention and execution which seldom fails. This is true even of his first short, *Hello,* made during the year he studied at the Film School. It is a comedy bagatelle about switched identities and sex-roles; a boy and a girl and a game with a wig. It is a film of light and movement, wit expressed in visual terms — exactly as in Jacques Demy, for instance.

Cornell started his artistic activity as a writer. He dropped out of film school after one academic year — for the possibility of making his first fiction film (a project which fell through) and in protest against the school's sub-standard teaching methods. After three feature films he has recently — partly as a result of the film crisis — been devoting himself to directing for the stage and television, especially interpretations of the classics: Strindberg's "Crimes and Crimes," Shakespeare's "All's Well That Ends Well," Molière's "Don Juan" and the Puccini opera "La Bohème."

Cornell's second and third feature films, *Like*

Night and Day and *The Pig Hunt,* also depict people trapped in patterns. Here it is the hierarchical structure of society that binds the individual. The main characters in both films, Susanne in *Like Night and Day* and the senior civil servant Siljeborg in *The Pig Hunt,* accept the class society, its form and its laws, and they move within the ifs and buts that clutter every step of the social staircase. Both Susanne and Siljeborg strive to climb without questioning the meaning or the methods of their efforts. Thus both *Like Night and Day* and *The Pig Hunt* are about lack of freedom.

Siljeborg is the totally bureaucratised man, a Head of Department in the State Livestock Inspectorate, with the task of exterminating all the pigs on the island of Gotland. He tackles his job with a zeal that excludes all criticism or imagination. He is a schizophrenic person, wholly adapted to the demands of a power system. There are perfectly watertight partitions between the private citizen Siljeborg, who is appalled by cruel experiments on animals, and the dutiful professional Siljeborg, attempting to solve his pig extermination problem with efficiency and technical inventiveness.

The picture of Susanne in *Like Night and Day* is more complex.

In a scene in *Like Night and Day* a guide is lecturing a group of students about the landscape gardening in the grounds of Drottningholm palace. He talks about the pattern formed by the flower-beds and the paths, about the perfect symmetry of the gardens. He sees their symmetry as the expression of a dream of what a society should look like: a society in which power is concentrated on a single point, diminishing the further one goes from the centre. But within this pattern, this strict symmetrical pattern, there is still a certain freedom of movement — that is, as long as one follows

Claire Wikholm and Agneta Ekmanner in LIKE NIGHT AND DAY

the paths, as long as one does not walk on the grass. . .

This is one of the film's key scenes. For Susanne this pattern is unconsciously a reality. She steers herself almost like a sleep-walker towards what she considers a centre, a goal in life. When she lets herself fall in love with her boyfriend's boss she is expressing a longing to change her social identity. And she dreams only of changing upwards. When she allows herself to be lured out on to the forbidden lawns she immediately loses control of herself and inevitably drops back to her point of departure. Since the values which she seeks to attain and defends are false ones, they can never offer her any support. Her lack of indepen-

dence leaves her a helpless prisoner in a rigid structure.

Susanne is a TV announcer. She lives with Rickard, a medical student. One day she meets Rickard's superior, the famous professor and brain surgeon Erland, who is newly divorced and wealthy into the bargain. Susanne exchanges her love for Rickard for an infatuation with Erland. Things start moving. Susanne marries Erland and moves into his villa in Drottningholm, which looks exactly like a feature in the glossy magazine she might have read last month. The whole thing is as banal as canned music, but this simplification and obviousness are intentional.

The story of Susanne could have finished here.

She has attained her new position. She is on a level with her most superficial daydreams. But this is only the starting point.

As in *Hugs and Kisses* a fourth person is introduced who upsets the pattern: Claire, Susanne's sister. One might see the sisters as two parts of the same personality, in which case Claire represents all that is pent up in Susanne, all the hidden emotional resources which Susanne does not dare own up to. Naturally Claire appears as a threat.

Claire challenges Susanne, enticing her to take a few steps outside the pattern. Claire gets her sister to sell some of Erland's shares, and while he is away on a trip abroad, the sisters start seeing each other more regularly. Rickard, too, is drawn into the picture. Susanne lets go of the almost programmed control she exerts over herself. She is led on into erotic games and a sort of childish irresponsibility. The consequences are of course, disastrous, as for all people who live in ignorance of the resources of emotions, dreams, and secret wishes which they carry unfulfilled inside them, inside the law-abiding personality they consider to be themselves.

Erland returns. He discovers Susanne's betrayal (as he must consider it). After an accident involving his son, for which Claire is possibly to blame (this is one of the film's mysteries) he gives Susanne to understand that he no longer wants anything to do with her.

The final shot shows Susanne convulsively weeping, aimlessly wandering around the maze-like pattern of paths in the palace grounds. The camera lifts high over the landscape and we see Susanne recede into the distance — a huddled figure in the rigid ornamentation of the park.

Cornell certainly goes "to meet reality with pre-determined patterns" in all the scenes of *Like Day and Night*. It is visually a very rich and exciting film, often with a delicately balanced mobility about the photography *(Like Day and Night,* like

Cornell's other films, was photographed by Lars Swanberg, his former film school colleague, who now heads the technical experimental activity at the Swedish Film Institute). The camera is never content with simply reproducing, but comments on the course of events.

This occurs, for instance, in the scene with Susanne's and Erland's wedding. The camera glides up the avenue towards the white country church, and when the bridal couple have emerged on to the steps and are being congratulated, the camera circles incessantly around the characters. In the more exalted scenes between Susanne and Claire and Rickard, when things start to get wild, Cornell employs a hand camera. And in the hospital wards and television centre the camera movements are more subdued. There is a tremendous visual inventiveness, but above all the visual language matches the content of the individual scenes.

Cornell's aesthetic does not impart an enhanced sense of reality but raises the film one step above reality. The director seeks to achieve this in the

Susanne pursues the ambulance at the end of LIKE NIGHT AND DAY

dialogue too, but here the film is in danger of losing its suggestiveness. Cornell works with abbreviations. He renounces the epic. Almost no changes of time or place are depicted, and every complex of scenes may be regarded as a separate chapter. Cornell deliberately rationalises the argumentation within these chapters. As we have already seen, he is not seeking "the truth," but *a* truth, and a highly subjective truth at that.

The dialogue is often strongly rhetorical, but since the images possess such powerful expressiveness the rhetoric is emphasised, and a kind of double objectivity results. The symbolism in a scene is simplified, becoming pretentious or running the risk of provoking ridicule. Cornell seeks to attain clarity, but the effect is sometimes one of excessive clarity.

One of the opening scenes of the film is a typical example of this. Rickard and Susanne meet in the television centre. They head for the exit. But the door is locked. They try the door next to it. That, too, is locked. Susanne tries to phone the caretaker but gets no answer. She walks out on to the empty floor.

"You know what," she says. "I'd like us to do something."

"We can't do anything," replies Rickard. "We've got to wait for the caretaker."

"I don't mean that," says Susanne. "I mean in general. . .I'd like us to *do* something."

"Do what?"

"Well, for instance. . . I don't know. I don't know. I don't know."

Cornell sometimes employs this rather sophisticated verbal embroidery, in which the dialogue goes round helplessly in circles. It is a pity, for when a minute later in the same scene Susanne declares, in quite a different tone of vehemence, her dissatisfaction, with Rickard, with herself and with the routine they live in, the words are in danger of sailing past us.

After Susanne's outburst Rickard goes up to the door and absent-mindedly touches the doorhandle. The door opens. It was open all the time!

Like Night and Day contains several similarly overworked sequences in which the various elements — dialogue, scenario, the symbolic import, the setting — detract from one another instead of heightening the feeling and the intensity of the scene. But this apart, *Like Night and Day* is distinguished by uncommon precision — and ambiguity. The beautiful glossy pictures of all the lavish but coldly repellent settings breathes an anguish which none of the exchanges of dialogue enunciate. *Like Day and Night* is a disturbing film, in many ways.

Cornell places things at a distance and brings them into focus. He studies behaviour with almost the same coolly impassioned researcher's zeal as Erland and Rickard show when examining one of their cases, a totally apathetic patient who lacks any ability to communicate with the outside world. Her reactions are only discernible in diagrams, which no one can decipher.

But the characters in *Like Day and Night* express themselves clearly, even though they are limited to words and gestures. Above all Agneta Ekmanner in the central part as Susanne. There is a nakedness and desperation about her acting which makes one immediately feel involved in the game to which she is exposed. She is a prisoner in her own dreams and in an inhuman landscape whose layout she has not yet had the strength to see through.

The final shot shows her paralysed by despair in the chastened labyrinth of the palace grounds. It is a pessimistic shot. But perhaps Susanne's drama is not finished here. Perhaps the shock can lead her towards freedom instead of destruction? And perhaps freedom can give birth to awareness, a first step towards change?

7 Films Are Just Great

Films are often more superficial than reflective. This is in the nature of the medium. To penetrate beneath the specious, superficial values and lay bare thoughts and emotions is therefore the film-maker's greatest challenge.

Jan Halldoff's films often move on the surface. He studies and depicts *milieux* and people, attitudes and gestures. He "imitates" the reality surrounding him. He eavesdrops on conversations — anecdotes, quarrels, jokes, discussions, confidences — and attempts to reproduce them with their face values, odours and emotions intact. He often talks of the importance of striking the right note in his films. This is why they tend to become sample-cards of moods and tensions between moods. People and situations are felt to be authentic — at that particular moment, in odd scenes and sketches. But they are not always felt to be real and soundly motivated as a whole. There is often a lack of analysis and consistency in Halldoff's films. He snips his way free from problems with a facility that is disquieting in the long run. His films are marked by nervousness and impatience.

Halldoff's relations with the cinema are also marked by restlessness. He is the most productive of the younger Swedish directors, and since his *début* with *The Myth* in 1966 he has darted from job to job. This poetically realistic *début* about a young man's quiet revolt against the social machinery was followed by the portrayal of youth in *Life Is Just Great,* and then by the pop-flavoured romance *Ola and Julia.* A controversial film about medical care, *The Corridor,* was followed by another outspoken effort, *A Dream of Freedom,* this time about juvenile delinquents, to which the black farce *Dog Days* constituted a sharp contrast. After a year almost exclusively devoted to television Halldoff came back with *The Office Party,* a look at modern day *moeurs* in comedy form, a dubious exercise in polemics, *Stone Face,* and a new farce, *The Wedding.* After these three heavily criticised films Halldoff made his most ambitious project, *The Last Adventure,* a penetrating portrait of a young teacher who falls in love with one of his pupils. The film is based on a novel by one of the most talented younger Swedish novelists, Per Gunnar Evander.

Halldoff was originally a photographer, of the self-taught kind. He readily admits to never having studied at a school of photography or read a book on the subject. He has acquired his technique and his knowledge empirically, as an assistant in a studio and darkroom and later as a freelance photographer. He has never studied at a film school either. . .

Halldoff was discovered as a stills photographer while working on Vilgot Sjöman's *491,* and he soon received more assignments in the cinema. He took the stills for Donner's *To Love* and Sjöman's *The*

Dress and *My Sister, My Love.* In 1965 he was suddenly given the chance to make two shorts, *Free Period* and *Nilsson*, two swift impressionistic portraits — the first about a schoolgirl and her experiences in a photographer's studio and bedroom during an hour off from school, the other an anguished and naked portrait of a suicide candidate about to make the definitive decision. Both films depict a concrete situation, limited in time and place. They both make a harmonious and accomplished impression. This limitation seems almost to be a prerequisite of success for Halldoff. Many of his other films, too, take place within a short space of time. *Life Is Just Great* and *A*

Dream of Freedom describe a couple of days in the life of the main characters. *The Office Party* and *The Wedding* are concentrated within half a day.

Halldoff's dilemma in relation to his films is best illustrated by his second film, *Life Is Just Great.* It might be called behaviouristic. It describes the attitudes and reactions of a small group of people during a few days in May 1966. The leading character in the film is a young woman, Britt. She is twenty-six, recently divorced, with a little son about five or six. A younger woman, Maj, perhaps seventeen years old, who babysits for her, introduces Britt into her gang (Thomas, Kent and Janne), and they draw her into games which she has not yet forgotten how to

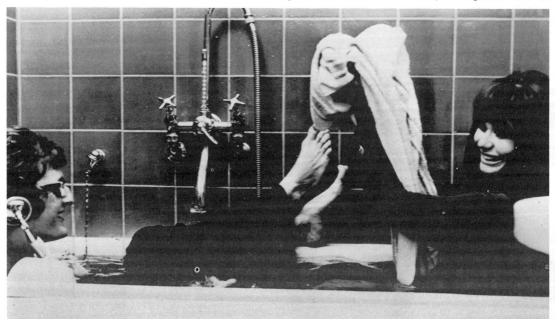

LIFE IS JUST GREAT, with Thomas Jansson and Inger Taube

play. Complications ensue — and pangs of conscience: there is Britt's job, from which she is taking time off, and there is Britt's ex-husband Roland, with his interfering observations and criticisms of Britt's life, which is really none of his business. And the game continues. The gang have a great time wearing stolen clothes, driving stolen cars and aping other people. Suddenly the game turns into tragedy. A man, a witness to one of the gang's more brutal pranks, dies. And Britt returns to her quietly humdrum existence.

Life Is Just Great is a film about the conflict between generations, about the clash of outlooks, but as an examiner of attitudes Halldoff seldom delves very deeply. He depicts the nihilistic apostles of the "lost generation," dictators in disguise with neither memory nor future, moving in an ideological vacuum and an emotional test-tube.

The provocations of the teenage gang in *Life Is Just Great* are blatant, insolent, obscene, defiant — according to the sort of people who are subjected to them. They are manifestations of a protest, but generally a protest for protest's sake, a protest lacking goal or direction. Maj, Thomas, Kent and Janne are drifting around in life, and only the provocations and confrontations give them any identity. Their actions are governed by impulse, and their impulsiveness can lead them as easily in a positive as in a negative direction.

It is easy to regard the actions of the gang from without, and characterise them as lax and mindless. This is how Halldoff lets the older generation view them, with Britt's ex-husband Roland in the centre. Halldoff presents these forty-year-old men in the first scenes of the film behind drained beer glasses in a high-class restaurant. It is an ironic introductory vignette that lends relief to the teenagers' rampages. The men round the bar-tables cough up their nausea and frustration in the meditative state that accompanies a hang-over. They are able to knock over glasses and chairs with

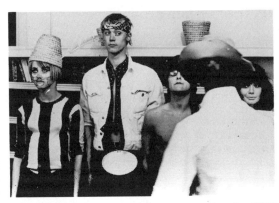

The dressing-up sequence in LIFE IS JUST GREAT

impunity. The head waiter promptly rushes over to put everything quickly right again. As usual the whole thing is a question of class and money.

The gang advances through a world of petty bourgeois entrenchments. Britt anxiously moves the worthless ornaments adorning her home and reacts vaguely against the gang's wild goings-on, while at the same time tempted by the intensity and lack of inhibition in their capers. But she is participating in a revolt at random. The aggressiveness of the youths — Halldoff does not shy away from depicting the cruelty of their games, the bullying and the compulsive gestures — has no conscious direction. The lack of moralising is a relief, but the lack of morality in the film is oppressive.

Life Is Just Great has a levity and musicality which are unusual in the Swedish cinema. But this levity is not always to the advantage of the film. It sometimes seems as if Halldoff is so careful to maintain the *tone* of the film that he forgets the characters. The gesture becomes more important than the action. The film is in many ways a piece of close-up reporting. Halldoff and his cameramen concentrate their attention on faces and details, and this sometimes threatens to obscure the overall picture.

It is an uneven film, with the rough patches clearly visible. There are obvious discrepancies between the written dialogue and the improvised conversations, between the more planned scenarios and handcamera exercises. A sort of indecision.

A specific example from the film may explain what I mean. After a visit to the funfair the gang gather at Britt's flat to continue their revels. The atmosphere is pretty lively. Thomas is lying fully dressed in the bath, which is full to overflowing, smoking and reading a comic. Britt catches sight of him through the open door and says, "Thomas, not with your trousers on!" Then Halldoff cuts, and in the next scene we see Britt also fully dressed, sliding down in the bath opposite Thomas. What has led her to do it? Halldoff shows a before and an after, but the critical (and interesting) moment when she makes up her mind is not depicted. The reaction, the opportunity to provide a motive, is cut out. Admittedly this speeds up the tempo, but owing to the faster tempo we risk losing touch with the characters, whom we should like to get to know better — particularly the main one, Britt.

And it is vital that we should be given the chance to get to know Britt. After all she is the hub of this tragi-comedy, around which the other roles revolve, however passive and easily swayed she may be. Halldoff himself has characterised Britt thus: "She is pliable but reacts against clumsy moves. She is young and her child is still more of a nuisance than company for her. She is lonely but does not suffer much from loneliness. She has never expected anything from inside herself, only awaited events from outside. She thinks well but not often."

Britt is vulnerable. She is exploited, at work, by her ex-husband, by the gang. But she is also exploited by Halldoff, the director. In the improvised conversations she always comes off worst. Neither Britt nor the actress Inger Taube has anything to say.

And so Britt functions throughout the film on the sidelines of the action, so to speak. Like Halldoff, she is no more than a passive observer, who after the shock of the final scene is able to run on towards new experiences.

* * *

Halldoff was better equipped when he came to make *A Dream of Freedom*. It is his most concrete and concise film. It is also, in my opinion, his best.

The film describes a couple of days in the lives of two young convicts. One has just left prison, the other is on the run. They meet by chance. The more dominant of the two inveigles the other into carrying out a bank robbery. During the subsequent hunt which is launched for them, a policeman is killed — knocked down by the fugitives' car. A witch-hunt is organised for these two "public enemies." Halldoff enables us in his film to get to know them both more closely — far from the sensational picture painted by the newspaper placards.

The film was inspired by a current legal case in Sweden, but this is irrelevant for our purposes. The pattern is only too familiar and typical of an oft-repeated reality, being justified — unfortunately — by its general validity.

The truth is concrete. Halldoff introduces his film with two personal case histories, in which two lives are summarised in the icily correct prose of bureaucracy:

Jan Henry Ravén, 410826-0513
Born in Oscar's parish in Stockholm, eldest of three children.
Parents: Henry S. Ravén, director, born 1917, and Ingegärd Emily (Emy) Barenkow, born 1916.

Anamnesis: normal. Intelligence quotient 156 (CVB).

Regular school attendance until matriculation examination 1961; good marks. Started to study law in 1962.

Has at times had unusually large amounts of money. Member of an illegal gambling club; large gambling debts. Cheque forgeries 1964. Unconditional sentence 1 year 8 months. Convicted again 1966, 2 years 6 months.

Deficient contact with others. Contact with father seems to be of unfortunate love-hate type. Father, who has become exceedingly wealthy by speculating in property, probably operates at times in direct breach of the law.

Highly talented but emotionally under-

Per Ragnar and Stig Törnblom on the run in A DREAM OF FREEDOM

developed. Organised — without getting personally involved — disorder and persecution of fellow prisoners and warders during his time in prison. Deep-seated need of psychological treatment.

Stig Emanuel Johansson, 431202-0083
Born in wedlock in Johannes parish, to Per Emanuel Johansson, haulier, born 1919, and Anna Kristina Lindgren, born 1920. Mother died (road accident) 1954. Father re-married 1957.
Anamnesis: normal birth and development, speech development possibly rather late.
Intelligence quotient (Wechsler) 104, non-verbal 112.
Regular school attendance until 1955, thereafter recurrent spells of truancy. Home breaking up. Theft of moped 1956. Taken in care for corrective training in February 1957. Placed in Folåsa approved school from Autumn Term 1957 until 1959. Brief vocational training (motor mechanic).
A number of shop break-ins 1961. Served prison sentence for these offences 1961-63, when he was released. Arrested again after two years for a series of office break-ins.
Conduct during prison terms extremely good. Favourable testimonials from all prison staff. A keen worker who performs his allotted tasks with good results. Friendly and seeks contact with others.
Authority bound, in need of guidance. Must be given priority with regard to work and accommodation, *in which case* prognosis good.
Temporarily released December 1968.
The *résumés* are brief but eloquent, forming an excellent basis for the film and for a closer acquaintanceship with the two main characters. These curt judgements are an expression of unwitting cynicism in their impassive correctness. They contains cold facts and assertions. There is no room for understanding or analysis. Jan is "highly talented but emotionally underdeveloped." Why? Stig is "a keen worker," he is "friendly and seeks contact." And so he damned-well should be! For eleven years he has been regularly taken into care by society's institutions, from approved schools to prisons, and he has clearly been conscientious and adept at conforming to the authoritarian demands of these institutions. These extracts are most expressive when it comes to Stig. Coming from such a poor background, he has never had a chance. This is, in fact, a theory which the film does not on the whole emphasise: that the laws are essentially class laws, which both in their formulation and application strike the lowest strata of the working class hardest.

A Dream of Freedom opens with Stig's release from prison. We recognise the routine from many other prison films, but the images are greyer. They convey neither drama nor hope, but merely state a fact. Nor is there anything to say that Stig is destined to cope particularly well outside the walls, nothing but his optimism, which receives its first dent when he meets his "guardian," a friendly and understanding but totally ineffectual contact in the free world. Stig has no job and no home. He has £7 in his pocket plus £13 food allowance for his first ten days of freedom. It is a couple of days before Christmas and Welfare Sweden is shutting for the holidays.

The film operates right from the outset on two levels. Partly the individual, in the portrayal of the two young men, and partly that of social criticism. The representatives of law-abiding society are ever-present, with their comments, analyses and cocksure points of view. There is the press, sacrificing Janne and Stickan in order to still our hunger for sensation. The whole gamut of a criminal's presumed behavioural pattern, according to the customary stereotypes, is offered to the already prejudiced public. There are the psychologists' defences and analyses, the police reports, the eye-witness accounts brimming over with exaggeration and delight at being in the centre of events, and there are the interviews with "the man in the street":

"Do you think we are too lenient towards criminals in this country?"

"Yes, we are a bit soft, I think."

"Do you think we should raise the penalty for murdering a police-officer, for instance?"

"Yes, I think we should."

"Do you know what the penalty is at present?"

"No, but I think they're too low, anyway."

After the *première* Halldoff was criticised because this part of the film contained too much routine material, consisting of well-known points of view. It was claimed that the description of society's reactions was as one-dimensional as the instant verdicts of the newspapers and the interviewees. And yet these views and this attitude are, after all, the prevailing ones! Public opinion is predominantly reactionary on these issues. The attitude to crime and punishment is still strongly repressive, and vengeance is a central theme in most arguments. So this glance at the actions of Janne and Stickan is important — as a contrast and as a commentary.

Janne and Stickan bear very little resemblance, then, to the figments of the newspapers and the general public. Halldoff lets us meet them, associate with them and get to know them. The portraits of Janne and Stickan are probably the most realistic and perspicacious this director has achieved, and he is greatly aided by two actors whom he has worked with on several occasions, Per Ragnar and Stig Törnblom.

The portraits of the more easily swayed Stickan and the dominant Janne are necessarily uncompromising. During these short days they are thrown back on each other, and we are left in their company. Masks and disguises fall away. Tough-

ness and confidence give way to irritation and weariness, and eventually to anguish and resignation. The comradeship between the two friends is threatened by the strains they are exposed to. The continuous friction caused by their enforced co-existence in conjunction with the nervous tension give rise to dissension. The external pressure provokes them to new desperate and criminal acts.

Halldoff depicts the relentless inevitability of the train of events in which Janne and Stickan are compelled to take part right up to their capitulation — which is no conclusion. For the tragedy, as *A Dream of Freedom* indicates, is of course that society's methods of rehabilitation and readjustment are fundamentally nothing but self-deception.

The dream of freedom is a myth. Somewhere inside, both Janne and Stickan are all the time aware of this. But nevertheless they drive their destinies inexorably forward to the line which society's guardians of law and order imagine they have measured out. *A Dream of Freedom* describes an unmasking. The film is a story about lost illusions.

Janne, the more aware of the two, sees his actions as a political protest. He opts out of a parental and social authority with which he is unable to reconcile himself. He therefore acts without guilt — rejecting society and the law — but this does not give him any sense of freedom, only a deeper sense of frustration and exclusion. He resembles the Faulkner hero, who, in the choice between grief and nothing, between life and death, chooses death, because death is the only sure refuge. His tragedy is revealed when towards the end of his narrative Halldoff brings a young girl into the plot. She surprises Janne and Stickan after they have taken shelter in a summer cottage:

JAN: Sit down! . . .could kill you.

ANN: I'm not afraid of dying.

ANN: What are you afraid of then?

ANN: Afterwards, when you're dead. I mean — I don't want to be packed into a coffin. With the lid nailed down, into the ground.

JAN: That'd be bloody marvellous! That'd be bloody marvellous!

ANN: Like a prison. . .not getting anywhere.

JAN: It's all over, for Christ's sake! Don't you understand?

ANN: I want to be free.

JAN: Marvellous, just burning up.

ANN: It's dark. You can't get anywhere, you're just there, you're. . .

JAN: Shut up!

Stickan's situation is in a way just as serious, since he lacks any awareness of himself. He accepts; he is meek. He is undoubtedly as compliant towards the warders in gaol as he now is towards Janne. Stickan is a member of society who conforms to its demands whether he is inside or outside the prison walls. As long as he has money in his pocket he functions normally. Stickan's tragedy is that he is never given the opportunity to confront himself with his ego — with his dream of freedom.

The story of Janne and Stickan is enacted in a landscape heavy with snow and darkness. The cold and the isolation from the outside world give the drama a sense of ineluctability. Halldoff avoids shots which might depict the landscape in an idyllic light. Instead, the white expanses convey panic and desolation. When the police helicopter swoops down to capture Stickan, who is fleeing over the ice in one of the film's final scenes, Halldoff keeps his camera at a distance. Behind the whirling curtain of snow we sense Stickan's capitulation. The capture of Janne is depicted just as brilliantly. He is on the crowded stands at an icehockey stadium. In a very wide long shot we see a couple of policemen approaching. The arrest is

Arrest in the snow in A DREAM OF FREEDOM

undramatic. The crowd of thousands does not even notice that Janne is being led away. All their attention is concentrated on the game. The symbolism of the shot is simple but eloquent. And over the loudspeakers a popular song comments ironically:

> . . . let's live our lives
> and see what happens
> love the time
> that life gives us. . .

Halldoff's productions are generally characterised by an aversion for complicated, mobile scenarios. This is a common sort of laziness in many younger Swedish directors. But in this case Halldoff's reliance on fixed camera angles turns out to be to the film's advantage. The camera remains objective, often regarding events at a distance, which endows the movies with stringency and a morality. There is a sort of artlessness about the images, an apparent lack of content and depth, which give them a documentary air; but these images are neither frivolously chosen nor flippantly composed. The grey-tinted photography convinces by its objectivity and simplicity — which in this case are simply synonyms for beauty and efficacy. Lars Johnson, who has gone "the hard way" and learnt his trade in the film industry, makes a significant contribution with his first job as director of photography.

The scenes of *A Dream of Freedom* are marked by exactitude and purposefulness; they are propelled onward by a determination that leaves no room for alternatives. Janne and Stickan are as good as lost right from the start. They know it, Halldoff knows it and we know it. They are unable to alter their reality. The responsibility rests on us.

A Dream of Freedom, with its immediacy and lack of illusions, is perhaps most strongly reminiscent of the many American films describing flights which lead nowhere but back to the starting point, films like Nicholas Ray's *They Live by Night* or Bruce Kessler's *Killer's Three*

It might be said that Halldoff's films are as good as the material on which they are based (the screenplay) allows them to be. Since his films lack any formal sophistication, any immediate stylistic consciousness — he seems to create his images "with his fingertips", by intuition alone — his proximity to the material is a major, in face a decisive factor. When Halldoff is simply being clever, catering for the presumed expectations of his audience, as in the pop melodrama *Ola & Julia* or in the farce called *The Wedding,* the result is disatrous. And when his social aspirations outstrip his ability and the depth of his commitment, as in *Stone Face,* embarrassment makes equally devastating intrusions among the pictures.

But when the themes of his films harmonise with a real personal interest on the part of the director, as in *Life is Just Great* and *A Dream of Freedom,* he creates a fine interplay between form and content. This also occurs in *The Last Adventure.*

Per Gunnar Evander, who wrote the novel on which *The Last Adventure* is based, would seem to be a writer who suits Halldoff. Evander, who is

Ann Zacharias and Göran Stangertz in *THE LAST ADVENTURE*

also unusually productive, tends to view his surroundings as if through a camera. His shots of Swedish government-offices and living-rooms are detailed and rich in observations. gesture, intonation, behaviour. Evander's stories are realistic, being firmly rooted in everyday life. But there are secrets and tensions behind the faithfully recorded dialogue. The dialogue lies like an ornate web over the ravines of silence and embarrassment which without this safety-net would threaten to gape wide-open. People talk so as not to reveal what they really think and feel, so as not to reveal who they really are. It is interesting to depict this complication on film, where glances and other body-signals are visualised and are able to supply contradictory information about characters who are politely conversing.

The Last Adventure describes social relations and milieux, in which communication tends to become ritualised, and conversations function as defences and disguises: the family and the social institutions — represented here by an army-camp and a school. The film expresses the fact that man is bound in his personal actions by certain generally accepted norms, stemming from his membership in society. For the main character of the film, the struggle consists in trying to break with all this dissimulation and find himself.

The hero of the film, Jimmy, finishes his national service. His plans for the future are hazy. He may get engaged. His girlfriend's demands are not put into words, but she is continually present as a silent, reproachful reminder. Though love is long since dead, their relationship has been going on for quite a while, and at times Jimmy tells himself that he ought not to let her down. Jimmy's mother, adhering more strictly to the proprieties, is more to the point: "Talking about getting engaged, Kerstin and I thought that Saturday would be a good day." His mother is eager for Jimmy to move home again ("It'll be cheaper that way"). All the insidious old arguments are wheeled out and brought to bear. All the ploys of emotional blackmail are used to disguise purely selfish demands. So Jimmy flees.

Perhaps Jimmy ought to have continued his studies. But he knows that if he opts for his studies this will cement his dependence on mother and girlfriend. So he takes a temporary teaching job to defend his autonomy.

The Last Adventure describes Jimmy's path towards a breakdown. Jimmy is unable to stand up to the pressure exerted by the repressivity of the family and institutionalised society. He refuses to submit, but lacks the strength to unravel the knots on his own. He withdraws more and more into himself, a prey to guilt and fantasy. He thinks he is going blind. When he meets the doctor at the mental hospital Jimmy introduces himself half-ironically, half-seriously as "Mattsson, depressive neurotic."

Halldoff depicts Jimmy's crisis with insight. In common with many modern psychologists, he sees society and the rigid norms for social intercourse imposed on us as the chief threat to the retention of a healthy personality-strengthening sense of identity. The repressive dictates of our authorities create anguish and schizophrenia. We live a life in which we are forced to deny many antural wishes and drives. A world of dissimulation is created, encouraging us to live behind masks. Illness permits an unmasking, the chance to find one's self.

The film centres on Jimmy's love affair with a young school-girl, Helfrid. She is a pupil of his, and he experiences a passion for her that throws him into emotional turmoil. She is the promise of a new age and a new freedom. Her view of love is generous, straightforward and natural. She is strong in her love because she knows that it is real and is enough for many. Love implies exchange, and is not tied down. But Jimmy cannot endure the freedom offered by Helfrid. He is too marked by the myths of the past. He *wants* to be tied down, to feel the security of dependence on another. He is unwilling to renounce the inheritance of demands, oppressive rights of possession and prudish laws which previous generations have decreed. He reacts with violent and exaggerated jealousy. With almost perspicacious lucidity he breaks with all the possibilities Helfrid offers. Jimmy gives himself up voluntarily to illness. Perhaps by means of it he may be able to go down and inwards toward a new starting-point. Perhaps this will be the last adventure — or a fresh start.

The Last Adventure conveys almost throughout a sense of truth and immediacy. Only in one or two cases do the portraits risk gliding into caricature. One of these is the picture of Jimmy's girlfriend. She is an all too perfect take-off of passive and eminently sensible yearning, a sort of apprentice housewife. Some of Jimmy's fellow patients virtually become stereotypes. Perhaps this is due to the fact that actors who are too well known have been allocated these parts. (The same phenomenon occurred in Halldoff's film about the health service, *The Corridor,* in which a number of famous actors were made to play some clearly over-pathetic patients. The actors turned out a few little antics or suffering miens in short and

Åke Lindström and Göran Stangertz in THE LAST ADVENTURE

echnically skillful sketches. But the results were cliches, and the film discussion would then sink to sentimentality or banality.)

But apart from these lapses, Halldoff has selected his cast with good judgement. The actors are simultaneously anonymous and representative, substantial and yet embodiments of an idea — Marianne Aminoff as the mother Åke Lindström as the headmaster Birger Malmsten as the captain. Nor does the psychiatrist risk becoming a film cliché of a psychiatrist. In Tomas Bolme's portrayal he is a very human, responsible character who shows both solicitude and seriousness. Göran Stangertz in the main part always expresses the emotional upheavals which rack Jimmy most convincingly. It is an intelligent and shrewd interpretation.

The Last Adventure is, in every respect, a film which involves its audience. It is in a film of this intimate, realistic format (like *Life Is Just Great* and *A Dream of Freedom*) that Halldoff displays his strength. Halldoff has been making films for ten years now. He has advanced from striking the right note to an understanding of people. Which is not bad at all.

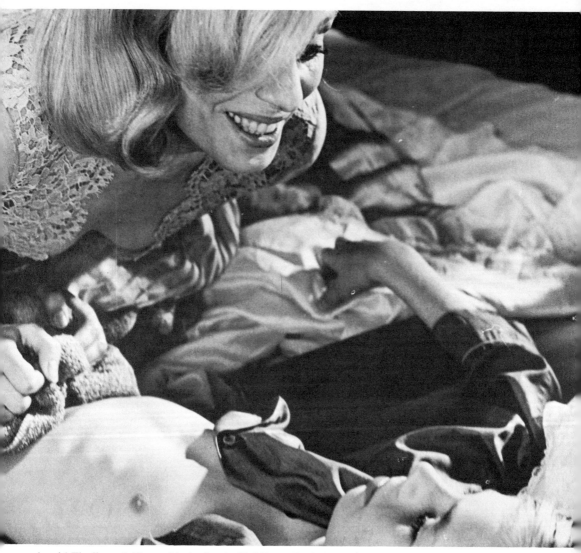

Ingrid Thulin and Jörgen Lindström in Mai Zetterling's NIGHT GAMES

8 Lonely Hunter

You sought a flower
    you found a fruit
You sought a spring
    you found an ocean
You sought a woman
    you found a soul
You were disappointed.
Edith Södergran

The great majority of films are still made by men. There is nothing original about this observation. For the entire world of art — and the same goes for politics, finance, industry — is still dominated by men; they are the planners, decision-makers, executives.

As a result, most of the major film portraits of women — the Mona Lisa or Madame Bovary of the cinema — are signed by men. This does not mean that they are devoid of insight or ability to identify. Catherine in Truffaut's *Jules et Jim*, Anita G. in Alexander Kluge's *Abschied von gestern* or Nathalie in Francis Ford Coppola's *The Rain People*, to mention a few examples, are all women who speak to us, but this does not stop us feeling that a complement is needed, a female view of these sisters and girlfriends.

But even the few films whose directors (note that this word has no feminine form) are women show a noticeably lukewarm interest in depicting social issues or problems of living together from a female point of view. It is true that in the films of Agnès Varda, for example, the women are the most richly portrayed of the characters, but if one studies any of the works of her female colleagues — Lina Wertmüller, Shirley Clarke, Liliana Cavani, Elaine May, Nadine Trintignant or Susan Sontag, to name a few of the more well-known women directors — there is often not much to distinguish their films from films dealing with similar issues but made by their male colleagues. One can, of course, point out a simple but not unimportant reason: the films of these female directors are invariably produced by men.

Yet even if there is still a lack of films dealing with the situation of women, reflected through female temperaments and perspectives, there are exceptions. Such as Marguerite Duras's *Nathalie Grenier*, Elda Tattoli's *Pianeta Venere*, Barbara Loden's *Wanda,* or collective films from the U.S.A., France, Germany, Denmark and other countries. Another exception is Mai Zetterling and her two films *Loving Couples* and *The Girls.*

Mai Zetterling returned to Sweden in the early Sixties to make her *début* as a director of fiction films. She had then spent two decades working as an actress, first in Sweden (in e.g. Alf Sjöberg's *Frenzy* and *Iris and the Lieutenant,* and Ingmar Bergman's *Music in Darkness*) and then in England (where she made her *début* in Basil Dearden's *Frieda* and went on to act in a score of English and American films). But Mai Zetterling soon found the role of actress too restricted and unsatisfying, and together with her husband, David Hughes, began to make documentaries for the BBC, including a couple of critical studies of Sweden, *The Polite Invasion* (about the problems of the Lapps) and *The Prosperity Race.* After her award-winning film *The War Game,* an allegorical fable about the mechanisms of war, starting with two little boys playing on a demolition-site, she felt ready for greater things.

Loving Couples is based on the series of novels by Agnes von Krusenstjerna called "Fröknarna von Pahlen," which Mai Zetterling and her script-collaborator David Hughes compressed into an *exposé* of the fates of three women. Agnes von Krusenstjerna was one of the most controversial female writers in modern Swedish literature. Like many of her female characters she lived a life in defiance of the conventions which others — with reference to her birth and sex — attempted to impose on her. Her suite of novels in seven volumes came out in the Thirties, and this great family chronicle, set in the years around the outbreak of the First World War, contains many autobiographical components.

Mai Zetterling's film — like the novel — regards events from the point of view of the women. Although the woman's world depicted is dominated by the men, her loyalty is all the time on the side of the women. It is the men who emerge as the weaklings, ruled by careers, conventions and a petrified emotional life. Most of them seem to speak in aphorisms. Words leave their bodies. Sentences are tied up and bitten off, and as the speech-bubbles ascend into the air the deliverer studies the effect of what he has said. In this Mai Zetterling makes admirable use of Gunnar Björnstrand's talents as a phrase-monger.

The men in *Loving Couples* have the function of the warders and prisoners of prudish, pre-industrial society. Admittedly they are the ones who make the rules and decisions, and of course ultimately the women fall victim to these unimaginative, repressed guardians. But the women are depicted as freer and therefore stronger. They are strong in their awareness, freer in thought and emotion. It is typical that the only man who is allowed to express fully spontaneous emotion and give his feelings both verbal and physical form is a homosexual artist.

Mai Zetterling's film has three main characters, Angela, Agda and Adèle. We meet them at the beginning of the film at the maternity hospital and their stories are related parallel to each other by means of flashbacks.

Angela belongs to the high-born family von Pahlen. From early childhood she is placed under the guardianship of the family, her parents having been killed in an accident. Her fairness and charm indicate sincerity and fragility, but these blonde qualities are also used by Angela as a protective mask concealing determination and will-power. Because of her sensitivity she discovers and reacts against the cold cynicism that is one of the most salient features of the people around her in the ancestral home.

Angela's childhood was a sheltered one. She was brought up as if under a bell-jar — on the family estate, at a girls' boarding school and finishing school. Yet she seems comparatively well equipped. Her self-confidence has been strengthened by the relation closest to her, Petra who also assumed the chief responsibility for her upbringing.

Agda is spontaneous and impulsive, hungry for the possibilities of life and love. She expresses her emotions long before she is sure they are the ones she possesses. She comes from a poor background and lives according to a simple but practical principle: that of giving and taking without losing on the deal. She is introduced into the von Pahlen family by the artist Stellan, for whom she poses. Her belief that love is free is not bassed on any emancipationist programmes, but she willingly demonstrates the honesty inherent in the theory for the men with whom she finds pleasure and joy. Agda becomes pregnant with a young officer but marries Stellan. This marriage of convenience amuses Stellan just as much as it does Agda. The fact that the couple do not spend their wedding-night together does not give either of them any particular cause for concern.

Adèle is the sombre and gloomy antithesis of Angela and Agda. She lives with the farmhand on the estate in a bitter and mute marriage. Adèle is the incarnation of frustration and disappointment. She meets her husband's signs of affection with corn. Ever since her insecure, poverty-stricken childhood she has reallsed where she stands in the hierarchy of the social scale. Adèle is a strong and impassioned human being, and this is her tragic dilemma. As a woman and as a representative of the proletariat she is so far down on the social ladder that she is unable to express her strength in any positive way, allowing of development. Hence she has a masochistic desire to see her strength overpowered, and she looks down on her husband who lacks the will or the ability to meet these demands. She regards the von Pahlen family with justifiable suspicion. She rejects their approaches, seeing through their attempts to buy themselves cleaner consciences *vis-à-vis* those they exploit. At Agda's wedding reception, to which Adèle and her husband are invited, she quite shamelessly screams out all her scorn and bitter-ness.

In the role of Adèle Mai Zetterling chooses sides: women's liberation is also a class issue. Angela and Agda dare to venture further outside the dreary rules of convention. Their self-assurance stems from birth, money or beauty. Adèle is inhibited by her poverty. It threatens her freedom on all levels.

By concentrating the narrative on these three women and setting their stories off against each other Mai Zetterling creates a complex interplay between ingenuousness and seriousness. *Loving Couples* achieves epic weight and social commit-ment. Moreover, the three women are regarded with the same degree of understanding. Adèle's vehement protest, Agda's flirtatious intriguing, and Angela's well-considered, rational decisions vir-tually convey three sides of a single personality. They form both a contrast and a complement to each other. But all three of them wage their struggles alone. Perhaps what is needed is the compound person which Angela-Agda-Adèle make up, if there is to be any possibility of more sweeping changes taking place in the direction of emancipation and social liberation.

Angela gives birth to the baby she is expecting

Eva Dahlbeck, Jan Malmsjö and Heinz Hopf in
LOVING COUPLES

with Thomas, a widower in his fifties who has previously courted Petra. Largely as a result of Thomas's breaches of promise, Petra has isolated herself and turned inwards on herself — a not uncommon fate among women. Petra is the victim of romantic love. Her self-confidence is so weak that when he — the only one — lets her down, her belief in love, a woman's primary means of self-expression at that time, vanishes too.

Angela does not marry. She will look after the child on her own — together with Petra. "Our child," says Petra, and when she embraces Angela there is no trace of jealousy or ambiguous intentions in the gesture. It shows loyalty — between women.

The birth of Agda's baby is less painful than in the case of Angela. She has been running and jumping up and down the corridors and staircases of the hospital in order to hasten the arrival of her "love-child". His future life will be unconventional, and this freer life-style may, perhaps, create a human being with better chances of breaking down obsolete attitudes and laws.

Adèle's baby is stillborn. There is no trace of symbolism or judgement about this fact. On the contrary, for each of the three women the ending is the most optimistic one and corresponds to their wishes. This, too, is an expression of loyalty to women.

"Men always let you down," is a line that is frequently heard in *Loving Couples.* Whether it is delivered with aggressive directness or forms an ironically introverted comment, it gives voice to a despairing awareness of abandonment and loneliness.

Loneliness is a central theme in Mai Zetterling's films. Human beings feel isolated, shut off, like living corpses; and in proportion to the increasing freedom in her films from a strictly formalistic style and "logical" structure, Mai Zetterling has

Ingrid Thulin, Jörgen Lindström and Lauritz Falk *in NIGHT GAMES*

striven with salubrious imaginativeness to illustrate this dilemma.

But these feelings are fraught with excessively fierce symbolism in the almost bombastic *Night Games,* in which the main character, Jan, seeks to come to terms with the nightmares of his past where his mother plays a dominating part. The film is acted out on two levels: partly in the present, partly in 1938, when the action centres round his mother's extravagant excesses in the company of a select band of spongers and gate-crashers which seem to have been borrowed from *Fantasia* or Fellini's surplus stores. No one could accuse Mai Zetterling of stinginess when it comes to this sort of thing.

Her film version of Hjalmar Söderberg's *Doctor Glas* is also marred by imagery that is far too heavy-handed and overloaded with symbolism. This intimate study of "the lust of the flesh and the incurable loneliness of the soul" — this classic phrase which Mai Zetterling could adopt as a motto for her films — is overexposed in more than one sense in the wide-angle treatment it receives from the camera of Mai Zetterling and Rune Ericson. As in *Night Games,* the anguish contained in the story is exaggerated by the anguish-charged visual presentation.

Perhaps Mai Zetterling's most disciplined analysis of the nature and terms of loneliness is to be found in her contribution to *Visions of Eight*, the documentary on the Munich Olympics. In it Mai Zetterling opted to study the weight-lifters, an unexpected choice, perhaps, but quite in line with her previous work. Predictably she had been asked by the producer to do a reportage on the women in the Olympics. Her choice of the weight-lifters might, in fact, be seen as a protest against the stereotype thinking of the producer. Mai Zetterling said that she wanted to tackle "the least obvious thing, that which is furthest away from what I am myself and am personally familiar with. When I planned the film I had two main headings in my notes — Loneliness and Obsession."

The Strongest is introduced by a short comment: "I am not interested in sport, but I am interested in obsessions." What follows is a penetrating study of the lives of these obsessed men during the time allotted to them for their appearance on stage: the involved and ritual preparations, the concentration, the total loneliness. For these actors standing there, confined in their bodies, which have had to withstand the most extreme strains in order to justify this appearance, have no support except from inside themselves, from their knowledge of the capacity of their own bodies. This sport seeks no participation from spectators or fans; rather, it demands an absence of spectators or absolute silence. They are artistes in free fall beneath the big top, actors who must not leave the circle of the spotlight or diverge from the text. All this is depicted by Mai Zetterling with respect and dignity — qualities which she is not concerned with observing too systematically in her feature films.

Mai Zetterling, who is also an actress, sees nothing grotesque or ridiculous in these over-proportioned bodies. They are the protagonists' stage-costumes, the essential prerequisites enabling them to perform the task they have set themselves out there in the arena. The director is on the side of the exposed and obsessed.

Mai Zetterling's most recent films, *The Girls, The Strongest* and *Vincent the Dutchman,* deal with the same problem from different vantage-points — the vulnerability and total solitude of the artist. And the recurring questions: For whom am I performing? Is it of any value? Am I getting through?

In David Hughes's book about the shooting of *The Girls,* Mai Zetterling says: "I want to be able to transmit an idea, a vision I have to the screen, to communicate with as many people as possible in this particular way. Perhaps it is conceited and smug to venture to think that one has something to say to a world, and it is hard sometimes, but I still carry on. I firmly believe and firmly hope that I shall succeed in creating *one* valid work of art that has something to say, to give. At any rate once.

"But I do not believe, as some people do, that a single work of art could change the world. Of course, artists have changed the world, but it usually takes time, sometimes even a whole generation or generations for something to penetrate. Artists often view politics in a semi-condescending way — they think it is degenerate and riddled with lies — and politicians naturally regard artists as naïve children who are mostly just a nuisance. But I think that there is a happy 'no man's land' where these things can mingle, just as Plato wished; artists and philosphers serving society together on a higher creative plane; men with visions. . ."

The Girls is the story of a theatre company on tour in Sweden with Aristophanes's "Lysistrata." The action revolves chiefly around the three actresses who play the leading parts in the play. They are Liz (Lysistrata), Marianne (Myrrhine) and Gunilla (Kalonike). They are played by Bibi Andersson, Harriet Andersson and Gunnel Lindblom. These are the three parts in the play, these are the three actresses in the film narrative, and as Bibi Andersson, Harriet Andersson and Gunnel Lindblom are three actresses with a very strong screen presence, somewhere along the line characteristics and views which are very much their own private ones are blended into the film.

The Girls is a satire on the man-woman relationship. The film naturally propagates women's liberation, but without using directly polemical means. In roughly the same ironical way as in Aristophanes's play the film depicts *les femmes faibles* in a critical situation. They wish to assert their rights but are uncertain as to their chances and the effective strength of their weapons. The protest in *The Girls* springs forth as a natural creation. It is spontaneous and emotional and is not poised on the secure springboard of political analysis. The girls react with anger and despair, defiantly and bluntly.

Mai Zetterling follows, in fact, a sort of logic of the emotions in the construction of the film. The main plot, which is already cloven — the rehearsals and performances of "Lysistrata," and the description of Liz, Marianne and Gunilla — is broken up by dreams, visions and sudden ideas.

Loving Couples was practically classical in its visual garb. In the deep focus shots, centres of gravity were distributed and effects apportioned. The sets were carefully thought out, showing a striving for balance and precision. The stiff formality characterising the world depicted was given a visual counterpart too. The camera frequently functioned as a natural centre towards which the acting of the participants was directed. As in the scene after the funeral of Angela's parents, when the camera captures and links up the grieving relatives in a circular panning shot. Or in the scene between Angela and Thomas, when the camera performs a 540-degree movement around a tree with the two main characters, while the whole of Angela's family pass review in the background as dumb witnesses. Occasionally one had the impression that Mai Zetterling had justified a scene by the brilliance and imaginativeness of its formal construction.

In *The Girls,* the reverse is true. The function of the photography is to give visual shape to the developing ideas as directly and polemically as possible. *The Girls* shows that Mai Zetterling controls the language of the cinema but refuses to allow herself to be controlled by it. Here, too, she is protesting — I can damned well dream how I like, can't I?!

As in *Loving Couples* the three central female parts in *The Girls* form contrasts and complements to one another. Liz lives with a stockbroker and two pugs. Liz and her husband are a decorative couple who undoubtedly do themselves credit in "fireside" interviews in glossy magazines. But their relationship is sterile and stuck in a rut. He criticises her professional ambitions, but at the same time finds them convenient. While his wife is on tour he has greater liberty to get together with his mistresses. Marianne has a child by a married

ibi Andersson rebels in THE GIRLS

an. Their relationship is being destroyed by his roken promises. Marianne also has difficulty in ooking after the child on her own. Much to the dignation of the male director she is sometimes rced to take the child along to rehearsals. unilla is married and has five children. Her usband is kind and considerate to the point of lf-effacement, but his "kindness" is also an

effective weapon when used against Gunilla's bad conscience. Gunilla is governed by her feelings of guilt, and her husband often drags in the children as an argument to lure her back to the (sometimes) calm haven of home. Gunilla flees from the clamouring demands of husband and children, finding the domestic idyll suffocating.

The three actresses analyse their roles in

Aristophanes's play, but never apply or translate the results to themselves. Gradually, however, their own desire for liberation reveals itself to them. Dreams, visions, memories and fantasies are depicted visually in grotesque, sardonic, farcical episodes. The victims of these sketch-like scenes are always men. They are stripped of their lies and tricked out of their complacency and selfishness.

In the character of Liz — who is the most complex of the three parts — there occurs a more profound identification with the role she is playing. Her protests, in words and actions, the most serious and aggressive.

Through Liz, too, the dilemma of the artist, the second central theme of the film, is depicted. She tries pathetically to break the isolation she experiences, but fails. One evening she steps up to the footlights and asks the audience to stay behind for a while to discuss the performance and the content of the play but is met by an embarrassed silence and a cynical comment from the male lead. And when she tries to establish contact with some ordinary people outside the theatre in one of the towns, and is invited home out of politeness by the head of the tourist office, she is greeted with bogus respect which barely conceals their suspicion and resentment. People do not expect her to step out of her role — neither her role in the play, nor her role as an actress, nor her role as a woman.

With increasing determination Liz takes the step over the footlights. She forces people to drop their masks and provokes confrontations. Behind the role there is an idea, a human being, needs, demands, hopes. Look at them!

When Liz senses that she is not getting any response to her views, her challenges become more violent and more desperate. At a press reception she tries to explain her attempts to communicate beyond the sealed-off roles trapping them all, but is stopped short by the preconceived opinions of the press. With sudden determination Liz begins to divest herself of her jewelry and her clothes. Her desperate strip-tease is followed by the entire female section of the theatre group. They hurl their clothes into the faces of the male audience — husbands, boyfriends, fellow actors, journalists — the passive onlookers. Mai Zetterling could no express more clearly than this what she wanted to say in *The Girls*.

The Girls, made in 1968, is Mai Zetterling's most recent feature film. Since then she has made an hour-long film called *Vincent the Dutchman*. It tells the story of an actor who arrives in Arles to play Van Gogh in a film. Like Liz in *The Girls*, he comes to identify more and more with his part. We see him walking across the poppy-fields and among the famous sunflowers, and while the actor is making himself familiar with this external reality, we are gradually thrust into the closed inner world of the artist. "This peculiar torture — loneliness," writes the actor in a letter shortly before he — like Van Gogh — commits suicide. Mai Zetterling offers us yet another fascinating study of loneliness and obsession.

Anyone desiring to make a film and having total liberty to choose his subject has two available alternatives. The decisive factor is his ambition. He may make a film about Judgement Day or about the final hours of a suicide case, about the ravages of capitalism or a love affair, about the Third World or about the situation of a foreigner in a strange country. It is all a matter of personality; the most important thing is, of course, that the film is a good one. The only decisive difference between the story about Judgement Day or about the suicide case is the degree of ambition with which the film-maker tackles his subject. There are certainly small subjects and large subjects, but a large subject is not necessarily of greater value than a small one. That is an illusion which can function as a trap. The basis of this theory comes from Claude Chabrol in an article which he published at the end of the Fifties. But the argument is still relevant and applicable.

Johan Bergenstråhle goes in for large subjects. His first film, *Made in Sweden,* is a satirical analysis of capitalism in Sweden, in which the self-righteous and unscrupulous policies of Swedish big business are contrasted to the poverty of the Third World. His second film, *A Baltic Tragedy,* is a reconstruction of an historical event, the extradition of 167 Baltic refugees to Russia in January 1946. In his third film, *Foreigners,* Bergenstråhle describes the situation of immigrants in Sweden. He does this by depicting the fortunes of a few selected people. This is Bergenstråhle's most concrete film, and also his best.

Made in Sweden attempts to span a considerable amount. On one level the film is constructed like a thriller in which capitalism with its all-powerful leaders and its faithful lackeys are the obvious villains. They constitute a threat not only to the hero of the film — the journalist Jörgen — but also to all the efforts of society to create a more just and more egalitarian world. The banking and industrial tycoon Magnus Rud manipulates money and men, controlled by a sole interest and aim: maximum profit and personal power. Of course, in the discussion with the press his motives may appear to be philanthropic, and we recognise the capitalist's alluring arguments: his company's plans for expansion will guarantee work for another so many people. That the development will have adverse effects for a considerably greater number of people is a fact that he naturally refuses to realise or discuss.

In one of the film's early scenes Rud calls a press conference: his company is planning to set up a subsidiary in Central America, based in Nicaragua and Venezuela. Rud naturally chooses to regard the company as supporting development in both of these countries; in short, it is dispensing a kind of aid. This is merely a front for exploitation in collusion with the rapacious policies of two reactionary governments.

Jörgen is given the job of investigating Rud's

activities in another of the developing countries, Thailand. Here, too, the Swedish company has allied itself in a similar way with the conservative government. But Jörgen also discovers that Rud's man in Bangkok is dealing in arms with the guerilla movement. Capitalism shows itself in all its degenerate ruthlessness. It seeks its allies everywhere where there is money to be made. It is its own religion and ideology. Here the film conveys a dizzy insight, a picture of capitalism as a "state within the state" which practises its own self-seeking politics — and foreign policy. For the dealings of capital in the foreign market constitute a *de facto* political action in blatant contradiction to official foreign policy.

While Jörgen's fact-finding continues, Bergenstråhle contrasts the poverty in the world with pictures of the prosperous country of Sweden. Documentary pictures from India and Thailand, pictures showing starvation and suffering, break into the idyllic portrayal of the Swedish welfare garden, where social democracy and capitalism extend their hands to each other across the negotiating table.

In a central scene Jörgen shows his girlfriend Kristina a film. It is a continuous loop of pictures showing deformed and mutilated human beings the victims of starvation and disease.. Time and

MADE IN SWEDEN: Lena Granhagen and Per Myrberg in Thailand

again the series of pictures is repeated while Kristina gets increasingly upset. Jörgen's theory is that you get used to suffering, and this enables you to take action. This is a doubtful hypothesis, for the film montage has the opposite effect. Instead one turns away from it, waiting for the show to come to an end; it has the effect of a cruel game. Kristina rounds on Jörgen and his film in furious despair: Why did he take the pictures, what is the point of them? In this situation the viewer sides with Kristina.

On another level of the film Bergenstråhle recounts the story of the love affair between Jörgen and Kristina — the small subject within the large one. It is the weakest link in the film — or rather the vagueness of all three levels combines to weaken the whole film. The love affair is a story with neither beginning nor end. All at once Jörgen and Kristina are in love with each other, and their love is depicted in a series of mundanely romantic pictures. Both Per Myrberg and Lena Granhagen in the two parts are true to life, tangible and spontaneous in thought and emotion — separately. But the description of love never really develops into anything but anaemic illustrations of a romance. Jörgen and Kristina wander through images smacking of fortuitousness and *Kitsch* in equal doses, without ever really communicating with each other.

The three planes of the film converge in a montage *à la* Lelouch, whereas the director had probably intended to create the same complex composite structure as in Resnais's *Hiroshima mon amour*. But the three levels function — or fail to function — completely autonomously, without affecting one another in a deliberate or meaningful way or reaching any kind of conclusion. It is true that the descriptions overlap. The commentary on the soundtrack is frequently made to contrast with what is being shown on the screen. Sometimes Bergenstråhle takes this method to such lengths that one is forced to spend a good deal of time in trying to unravel the identity of the various voices. This creates an ambiguity synonymous with obscurity.

It is a shame that Bergenstråhle blurs the impact of his ideas in this way, for the film deals with important issues. *Made in Sweden* is a very ambitious film, but the ambition falls between three stools. And in spite of the unusually rich flow of images, the upshot is merely a colourful emblem, not unlike the multi-coloured badges bearing slogans which we pin to our lapels.

A Baltic Tragedy takes up one of the most controversial juridicial cases of a political nature in modern Swedish history. At the request of the Soviet Union, and after acrimonious debate in the press and in parliament, 167 Baltic refugees were deported. They had voluntarily enlisted in the German army or been forcibly conscripted, and fled from their homelands with some 3,000 of their countrymen on the conclusion of peace. In Sweden they were interned in camps. In November 1945 the government announced that all 167 were to be extradited. Violent opposition broke out against the decision and the internees protested with hunger strikes and suicide attempts. But on January 25, 1946, 146 of these legionaries were extradited to Russia. Of the other 21 men, some had committed suicide, some were injured as a result of self-mutilation, others were too ill to travel.

These are the events related by Bergenstråhle, but in this film too his intentions are obscure. On the one hand he presents an account of camp life in which individual destinies are portrayed with shocking dramatical intensity — suicide attempts, self-inflicted mutilation, tense confrontations fraught with such emotional force that they cannot fail to affect the audience. These scenes provide incontestable proof that the Swedish government acted inhumanely and that the opinion in Sweden against extradition was right. Something else which goes to emphasise the director's commitment to the cause of the Balts is his way of depicting the Swedes who appear in the film. The camp staff and guards are either innocents totally unaware of the drama being enacted or just working callously to order.

Bergenstråhle mixes fiction film sequences with documentary material and newsreel footage, with maps, statistics and diagrams, while a commentator's voice tries to give a more sober and balanced presentation of this complex of problems. In this more factual part of the film, reasons are advanced to justify the decisions taken by the authorities. What was the fate threatening the internees? The Balts feared the death penalty. After all, they were war criminals and had betrayed their country. We are informed that the Balts' fear was exaggerated. We learn that the majority of those deported were allowed to leave the Russian transit camps as free men less than a year after their return to Lithuania. Only about twenty received sentences of several years' imprisonment. Why then, was public opinion whipped up to such a pitch? In 1946 the Cold War has already entered its first phase. Terror of the Russians is one of the new inventions of reactionary opinion.

By approaching his subject from various different angles, Bergenstråhle tries to achieve objectivity, but all the same, the result is not the intended one. No objective reasoning under the sun could have the same force of impact as shots of blood and violence appealing directly to our humanity and compassion.

In one scene a priest performs a war wedding, saying that in the collision between political decisions and living people, he always sides with the human being. If the priest serves as a mouthpiece or alibi for the director then all possibilities of reflection and reasoning have been nipped in the bud by means of a shabby trick. The stance adopted by Bergenstråhle shows a lack of awareness which is dangerous, for even if all opinions are presented, in the form he has given it *A Baltic Tragedy* is an invitation to involvement without responsibility.

Foreigners, like *Made in Sweden* and *A Baltic Tragedy,* tackles a "large" subject: the immigrant situation. But this time Bergenstråhle has selected a more personal perspective for his treatment. *Foreigners* is a down-to-earth yet sensitive account of the life of a group of Greeks in Sweden. It recounts a story that is unusually warm, human and moving; Bergenstråhle copes successfully with the intimate format and the close contact with his handful of people. He does not need to demonstrate any overweening ambitions. It is sufficient for him to keep pace with a story that breathes life with a natural rhythm of its own.

Like Bergenstråhle's two previous films, *Foreigners* is based on a literary antecedent, in this case an autobiographical novel of the same name by a Greek immigrant, Theodor Kallifatides. In this film Bergenstråhle has stuck much closer to the original, presumably out of practical necessity: as a non-Greek he must have been more dependent on the nuances, the colour and the earthy language of the novel. Furthermore, the original novel already possesses an almost cinematic immediacy.

The main character, Stelios, has recently arrived in Sweden, and lives with a number of his countrymen in a rundown flat in a working class part of Stockholm. They are a strangely assorted group. There is Tomas, a disillusioned fellow getting on in years who works as a washer-up in a restaurant. There is Maria, who works in a factory but dreams of a future married to a Swede and integrated into the Swedish welfare state. There is Kostas, who after being sacked from his factory job tries to get by in various (not always wholly legal) ways. And there is Dimitris, who constantly has two or three jobs on the go at the same time.

He dreams of one day returning to Greece as a rich man, with an impressive dowry for his sister. Above his bed hang newly purchased suits in neat polythene bags.

These four characters constitute a virtual cross-section of "typical immigrants" and their fortunes. But the point is that they never strike us as examples, but as extremely lively people. We are induced to identify with them, with their hopes and dreams. Through them we are also forced to see Swedish society with completely fresh eyes. To see it as does the stranger who is met with suspicion and benevolence, by the coldness born of shyness which may at times break out into aggression, or by generosity whose obverse may reveal exploitation.

Foreigners is a very funny film. The humour which pervades it is both burlesque and of a quieter kind. Much in the film is seen through the astonished eyes of the newcomer Stelios and is thus magnified and distorted.

Stelios gets a job washing up at the same restaurant where Tomas works. He becomes the manageress's pet and quickly advances to bartender. But at the wild crayfish-party which the manageress gives for the restaurant staff, "sweet little Stelios" refuses to respond to her far from discreet advances. He is demoted, and before long the manageress finds an excuse to give him the sack. In a hilarious and very Greek scene, however, Stelios returns to the restaurant to take his revenge.

Foreigners is based to a large extent on moods. There are continual abrupt switches from hope to desperation and despondency, from poetry and sensual joy to nausea and despair. The comedy always goes hand in hand with seriousness.

Stelios experiences the disappointment that comes of feeling exploited, both at work and in his relationship with a young Swedish girl. Maria's dream of love is cruelly dashed in her encounter with an unfeeling and immature Swedish Romeo.

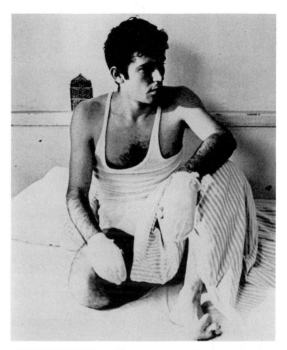

FOREIGNERS: *Konstantinos Papageorgiou as Stelios (above), and Maria Antipa as Maria (below)*

And Tomas, who has long been plagued by illness, dies in this strange country, which has never really regarded him as anything but an exotic outsider.

There is often a sort of melancholy beauty about the film. One readily remembers an episode in which the little Greek colony makes its way into the country outside Stockholm. It is early summer and all is lush and green; they sit down in the grass and drink retsina. Maria and Kostas's girlfriend Despina spread out the meal while the three younger men kick a ball about. These scenes convey a picture of a sensual *joie de vivre* and a simultaneous isolation. The Greeks are cut off from their tradition and their identity in this blond landscape so unlike their own. Suddenly old Tomas is stricken with bottomless despair and a wild, vehement longing for the country which he is never to see again. Sweden provides constant reminders — of qualities of life which it lacks.

For Stelios and his friends will always remain outsiders. Though the Swedes may invite the foreigner to dine at their table, they often do so. out of charity or a sense of duty. The foreigner takes what he is offered, while his hosts leave the table. They have done their duty, after all. They do not realise that their guest may have desires and needs beyond the purely physical ones. Contact, friendship, warmth. *Foreigners* is also a film about loneliness, about people's inability to get through to one another.

Of course the fact that the characters in *Foreigners* come so close to us and are felt to be so important is also due to the cast. With one exception they are all amateurs from the Greek colony in Stockholm. In their different ways they all lend dignity to this human comedy.

Bergenstråhle is primarily a theatrical director — he has directed a series of masterful interpretations of Brecht plays ("Saint Joan of the Stockyards", "The Caucasian Chalk Circle," "The Good Person of Szechwan") and has dramatised a number of classic Swedish epic novels, as well as some very stringent television plays (Strindberg's "Ghost Sonata" and "Gustav III," for example). Perhaps he considered this film in the small format a more challenging task than his two first films. In the case of *Made in Sweden* and *A Baltic Tragedy* he seems to have been the victim of the ambition to create Cinema and exploit all the means of the medium at once. *Foreigners* proves that ambition and outcome are not dependent on the magnitude of the subject — quite the contrary.

10 The Search for Perfection

Roy Andersson is the youngest of the more recent Swedish film directors. He is also one of the more aware, and technically one of the most skilful. His films are made with seriousness and knowledge. Their maker displays an almost fanatical desire for perfection. This has given the films a seductively beautiful surface. But their carefully devised and executed plot structure and composition do not merely reveal aesthetic refinement. The knowledgeable surface conceals complications and disturbing tensions.

Roy Andersson made his first feature film in 1970. Shortly before this, he had finished film school and collaborated in the collective film about the demonstrations against the Davis Cup match between Sweden and Rhodesia, *The White Sport.* His *début* film, *A Swedish Love Story,* became the big Swedish film success of the year. It was a gently poetic and yet firmly down-to-earth story about two very young people's first love.

A Swedish Love Story might just as aptly have been called *Sweden 1970.* The film stood in the centre of our prosaic day-to-day life, registering and recording it. *A Love Story* dwelt just as much on the adults surrounding the teenage lovers — parents, relatives, parents' acquaintance. The film created a Swedish microcosm in which Andersson with insight and sympathy studied human relations and behaviour.

Even in the very first shots the film gets a firm grip on the everyday life which Andersson seeks to depict. We are in a garage workshop. The last jobs of the day are being finished off. Pay packets are being handed out. With earthy humour some of the mechanics describe how they intend to spend the weekend. In these spontaneous exchanges the tone of the film is set. The garage door is flung open. Outside there is sun, summer, freedom.

The opening build-up in *A Love Story* is brilliant. We are whisked off to the grounds of a hospital. It is very early summer. The grounds are embedded in lush, tender verdure. The strong early summer light washes down over the surroundings. It is a harsh light which bleaches the already brittle hues of nature. This harsh light gives birth to both hope and anguish in equal measure. The summer light creates dreams of fulfilment. It is life-approving. It betokens longing, flowering, presentiments. . .

The people strolling around the grounds, chatting cheerfully with flowers in their hands, also seem to be possessed by the feelings which the light arouses. But, this almost idyllic paradise emanating from the images is treacherous. The light also implies a threat. It seems to make deadly demands of the people staying at the hospital, the discarded ones, those who do not dare to meet the cry for rebirth which the light conveys. They hesitate until the last minute to leave the dark security of the hospital corridors, and hide beneath the protective shadows of the foliage during the encounter with relatives paying their

A SWEDISH LOVE STORY

Ann-Sofie Kylin in A SWEDISH LOVE STORY

Anita Lindblom in A SWEDISH LOVE STORY

regular visits.

Here, in the hospital grounds, Andersson brings together the two main characters of the film, Pär and Annika. They are both around fourteen or fifteen years old, having come with their families to visit relations of theirs being treated at the hospital. The relatives are Pär's grandfather and Annika's aunt, two lonely, abandoned figures in the middle of a noisy, almost obtrusively carefree family union.

In his studies of schizophrenia and his analyses of family life, R.D. Laing has developed the theory that the family unit often, unconsciously, selects one of its members as a conductor for the crises that arise within the collective. On this person tensions and conflicts are projected. The chosen member becomes a receiver and a filter for all the clashes which arise within the group. He or she is made to act as a pair of scales or a watershed in order to maintain the necessary equilibrium between the relationships. In serious cases the tensions may be so grave for this reluctant scapegoat that they can lead to schizophrenia. The tensions within the family group and towards the person who is forced to act as a conductor also reflect the tensions aimed at the group from without, social demands and obligations.

The grandfather and the aunt in *A Love Story* have these victim roles. The families which cluster around them radiate harmony and cohesion largely thanks to the presence of these two invalids. The apparent harmony is a defensive attitude *vis-à-vis* those who have been excluded, a false assurance of security, and this very fragile *facade* is liable to crack at any moment. The confrontations here are full of shame and guilt and duty. Attempts to create a natural, intimate contact fail. The meetings are an embarrassment for both parts, a reminder of their failures.

In the midst of this atmosphere of benevolence and encouragement the isolation and desperation of grandfather and aunt are clearly discernible. Both react with a sudden vehemence which disturbs those around them and for a while upsets the apparent balance they are trying to maintain.

The aunt has a fit of weeping. Her sister clumsily tries to comfort her, or to make her show her anguish less publicly. Mechanical, solicitous instincts take over, as impersonal as those of the nurses.

Pär's grandfather breaks into a despairing and emotional monologue in which he voices with great bitterness his disappointment at the loneliness and estrangement of old age: "Today's life isn't built for me... It isn't built for lonely people... Once we thought that life would be equal for all — but it isn't. Did you hear?" A mocking aside from a fellow-patient casts light on the betrayal which he feels society, too, has committed: "Just you wait until we get a social democratic government. Then everything'll be all right." The dream of a society for everyone, a society with justice and fellowship is just an illusion.

Roy Andersson carries out his analysis of the conflicts with both shrewdness and tenderness. He regards the confrontations from a distance, and at the same time succeeds in creating a feeling of understanding. This feeling is extended to all those involved. They are all trapped in their ways, with their different casts of mind and their unfulfilled dreams and hopes. They are incapable of any deeper commitment — at present.

The whole sequence is full of observations and sounds which reinforce the lack of contact. The confused meetings between the patients and relatives, the irritations while queueing for refreshments, a dog getting tangled up in its lead, children crying, the discordant notes of a flute which a little girl is trying to play. And surrounding all this, the open, free, harmonious landscape which is the scene of these desperate attempts to get closer to each other.

In this atmosphere pervaded by frustration and desperation the film's two young lovers meet. They fight their way free of the adults' mechanical and prestige-bound demonstrations of convulsive gestures and non-committal conversations. For the present, at any rate, Pär and Annika are still free. They are able to meet each other's glances, with shyness of course, but without dissimulation. They are halfway between the worlds of the child and the adult. They have the spontaneity of the child but also the seed of the adult world's role-play, though as yet only a feeble imitation.

Andersson has fashioned their love story almost as a paraphrase of "Romeo and Juliet." When Pär and Annika eventually see each other again, the obstacles in the way of a meeting seem almost insuperable. They belong to different gangs, and to overstep the boundaries of the gang domains seems to be impossible. The prelude to their union is a game on the gang's terms. All the time they are obliged to mask their emotion in front of the gang.

The two parties despatch couriers as go-betweens and negotiators. The whole thing becomes an almost ritual game. There are many misunderstandings and obstacles before contact is first made. The gangs have their laws, which are much more rigid than the ones adults use to protect themselves. Their infatuation assumes the force of a passion in a classical drama. It is a matter of life and death for them both.

Both Pär and Annika surrender to their passion with all the bittersweet, complacent gush of emotion which a teenage love may command. There are many notes between hope and despair for them to strike, and Andersson uses the whole scale.

Pär and Annika have no language with which to express their emotions. They communicate by means of hidden signals, a sort of sign language of the body and eyes. Much is conveyed by demonstration. When Pär roars past on his moped it has the function of a virility symbol. "You have to be hard," says one of his mates. Annika hides behind female attributes, mirror and make-up. Andersson consistently shows a keen eye for this secret language of gestures and attitudes.

Even in the decisive sequence which eventually unites the two of them Andersson maintains a romantic, almost theatrical perspective. Pär and his friends leave the football pitch on their mopeds. Annika suddenly steps out of her passive role as an ostensibly indifferent onlooker and rushes after them. But Pär pretends not to see her and disappears over a rise. Annika stands there abandoned in the centre of the big gravel pitch. She weeps with despair and desolation. Suddenly we see Pär approaching on his moped far away in the distance. He looks like a Western hero racing across the prairie to meet his sweetheart. He swerves up on his moped in front of Annika, throwing himself from the saddle. The moped falls to the ground and lies there, engine running and wheels spinning. Pär and Annika embrace. Now the camera zooms back, revealing Annika's best friend and go-between behind the enclosure. In tears she observes the scene through the wire netting. By letting this minor character witness the union of the lovers from the wings, Andersson charges the scene with even greater emotional force. It is a way of reinforcing a feeling, a brilliant sentimental gesture that comes off.

Time and again Andersson finds pictures which immediately capture the tone of an emotional situation. Since Pär and Annika never put their feelings into words and their gestures are so often clumsy, atmosphere and emotion have to be conveyed through the medium of the picture. An instance of this might be the jubilant camera ride as Pär speeds home on his moped at dusk after one of his first encounters with Annika. Or again, the momentary image of an elbow along the edge of the balustrade as Pär and Annika are walking along a railway bridge. And all the time there is the music, commenting and guiding with melancholy or joyful ballad verses.

Running parallel with the story of Pär and Annika is a description of their parents' lives. With the same richness of perception Andersson executes his analysis of the more mechanical and norm-ridden existence of the adult world. Annika's parents, in particular, are ruled by the social conventions, of which career-hunting and status-seeking are the most firmly imprinted re-

Bertil Norström as John in A SWEDISH LOVE STORY

flexes.

Annika's father is a refrigerator salesman. He has worked his way up in society, and is fanatically afraid of slipping down a notch on the social scale. He is the faithful retainer of commercialism and capitalism. His car is his dignity, a token of success and social prestige. When some children accidentally kick their football on to his cherished status symbol he descends on them with an excess of aggression that merely reveals his deep-seated insecurity. Self-confidence and self-esteem have no natural grounding. These traits derive from material attributes. Annika's father has been deformed in the course of his strenuous battle to attain a position in society. His anxiety is an expression of the imcompleteness and impoverishment of his own personality.

His wife seems to be a more powerful personality, but in her too there are traces of the same sort of deformation. Love has been worn out by marriage. Dreams and hopes have foundered in the daily routine. She compensates for the futility and vacuousness of life with a new fur-coat and plans for a new flat. For her, too, personal fulfilment is a question of bank balance.

Annika's parents are like two perfect actors who never muff their lines. In a fiendishly ironic scene Andersson assembles the family at a congress at the refrigerator company. A new model is to be launched and old servants of the firm gracefully pensioned off. Directors and retailers sing their praises (Annika's father sweating with nerves at making this important official appearance), and the relatives pose proudly and loyally in their seats. Annika and her aunt are the only odd ones out, distracting and inattentive spectators at this demonstration of commercialism's programmed lack of contact and utter emptiness. It even sounds like a string of advertising slogans when the participants are talking among themselves, and the occasion is rounded off by a dutifully sincere rendering of the national anthem by all those present. It is a deadly accurate, and — by virtue of its earnest solemnity — a tremendously comic scene.

But frustration breaks through this thin veneer as soon as the occasion arises. One day Annika's aunt's male friend comes to visit them. He is a disturbing incidental figure; in a few short glimpses Andersson indicates his sadistic behaviour towards the woman with whom he lives. Even in this love relationship she has assumed the role of victim.

The family is getting ready for an outing. They are all busy and the atmosphere seems harmonious. But as soon as the visitor arrives the tensions are exposed.

FRIEND: What sort of car have you got?

ANNIKA'S FATHER: A Peugeot, why?

FRIEND: Lousy car!
   What about your job?
ANNIKA'S FATHER: Not bad.
FRIEND: Wrong business!

Suddenly the fight is underway. Bitter words shatter the apparent concord. All the hidden aggressions which the parents have been nursing come out into the open. *A Swedish Love Story* is a profoundly illusion-free account of everyday life. Among the chief merits of the film are the psychological insight and truthfulness which permeate every moment of the story.

Pär's father has a more secure footing in reality. He owns a garage and has a couple of employees. He is satisfied with life, and when he yields from time to time to his wife's status-seeking — which is not particularly serious or far-reaching — his efforts develop into comic pirouettes (such as the futile attempt to put up a pair of swing-doors between the hall and the living-room of their house).

In the film's concluding crayfish party all the characters are brought together. Pär's parents have invited Annika's family to their summer cottage. The crayfish party, this traditional Swedish social event with its almost ritual ceremonial, forms the backdrop for a final reckoning with the short-comings of the adult world. Here, too, the stage-props are a protective disguise: the hats, the lanterns, the drinking songs, the dinner ritual. But their well-brought up social attitudes collapse as the *schnaps* begins to tell. Annika's father, having been the target of the others' ridicule all evening, suddenly loses his self-control. Hysterically laughing, he disappears from the party, yelling out his frustration, cursing the others for the betrayals he has perpetrated on himself. Suddenly the others come to their senses. They are afraid that the missing man may have drowned or tried to drown himself. During their search Andersson keeps his camera at a distance, and their desperate hunt is given an unexpected air of absurdity. One may easily place a symbolic interpretation on the revellers' pathetic search in the thick mists around the cottage.

During the party Pär and Annika almost imperceptibly drop out of the action. We see them watching from a distance the ignominious home-coming of Annika's father. They are free, pro-tected by the happiness and warmth of their love — for the while.

A Swedish Love Story is a rich and accom-plished study of everyday life, full of humour and ironic observations. The film is packed with incident — and experience. Its realism is absolute, and even its more bizarre elements have a sur-prising tangibility. It displays an uncommon intimacy with the fortunes of its characters, and Andersson's formal freedom of movement is con-siderable and unhampered. His images are tremen-dously precise in their documentation of everyday trivialities and yet at the same time fraught with sensuality. *A Swedish Love Story* possesses some of the same lyrical realism that characterises Widerberg's films. Andersson also shows his sensi-tivity in his collaboration with the actors. Ann-Sofie Sylin and Rolf Sohlman breathe life into the pair of young lovers with natural ease and gentle-ness. And the popular singer Anita Lindblom, in her first dramatic role, brings a raw vulnerability and thoroughly genuine despair to the complicated portrait of the neurotic aunt.

A Swedish Love Story, is, alongside Vilgot Sjöman's *The Mistress,* the most confident film *début* in modern Swedish cinema. It is unusual to find such highly developed sensitivity in such a young film-maker (Andersson was only twenty-seven years old when he made the film).

* * *

Four years have now elapsed between Roy

Andersson's film *début* and his second feature, *Giliap*. The delay was caused neither by dearth of ideas nor by fear of possibly exaggerated expectations after his successful *début*. Andersson believes in precision, planning and organisation. There are few Swedish film directors who take a more professional view of their trade. It is also an artificial demand to expect an artist, in whatever field he may work, to produce a new work every year as a matter of course.

And *Giliap* is a film which required preparation. The screenplay took a year to write. It is very exact in expression and intention, fraught with moods and tensions.

Giliap was mostly shot in the film studios, which is something very unusual in Swedish cinema at present. But Andersson felt that he could not progress any further with the method he employed in *A Love Story* of shooting the whole thing on location. He wanted to develop his command of the cinematic language in *Giliap,* and by working in the studio he was able to practise a more elaborate camera technique.

Giliap is a very odd story. Or rather, it deals with unusual people in an extremely everyday setting. There is a powerful and highly charged contrast between the familiar *milieu* which the film depicts and the people who work there. *Giliap* is set in a hotel and its main characters are members of the hotel staff. *Giliap* deals with essential existential problems concerning the conditions of human life, but Andersson considers that these vital issues need not be presented in intellectual surroundings or formulated by representatives of intellectual occupations. On the contrary it is important to deal with the serious side of life through people with ordinary jobs, in order to demonstrate the general nature of the problems.

Giliap is a nickname assigned to the main character of the film. It originates from one of the countless authentic or fictitious stories about the organised gangster world in America during the Twenties and Thirties.

In the presentation of the screenplay Giliap is characterised as a man about thirty. He turns up at the hotel one day to start a job as a waiter. He is a stranger in from the unknown. He is not a waiter, though he has some experience from previous odd jobs at sea. Nor is he a seaman.

Giliap has had so many different jobs that he does not really know who he is. Nor has this ever worried him. He has always had life in front of him, or so he thought. In time he would make up his mind and find something that gave him a sense of fulfilment. The hotel job is just an emergency solution to provide him with food and ready money while waiting for something better. He is travelling on, out into the world, away.

The man who gives him his nickname is Gustav Svensson, called the Count. The Count works at the hotel but despises his job. He sees his work as a platform from which to carry out his plans, in accordance with laws which he himself has laid down. He feels ill-used and spurned by life, longing for a life with self-esteem and money.

The Count has decided to take what he has not been given, and take it with violence. This is to be done with the help of an organisation in which he is the self-appointed and supreme leader. He intends to stage one great *coup* which will enable him to lead a carefree life with self-respect and status.

The third main character is a young woman, Anna, who works at the hotel as a waitress and with whom the Count is in love. We do not know if she has an erotic relationship with him, but she feels sorry for him, and experiences a sort of filial security in his presence.

The Count recruits Giliap into his gangster syndicate, and even though Giliap realises that the Count's plans are crazy, he goes along with them.

Giliap also loves Anna, and she loves him. The relations between these three characters form the film's high-tension field.

As in *A Swedish Love Story,* everyday life is the starting point for the drama which Andersson enacts in *Giliap.* When the main character arrives at the hotel, preparations are in progress for a funeral dinner in the hotel dining rooms. The staff are laying the tables and preparing the buffet under the supervision of the manager, who is confined to a wheelchair. He appears as a sort of Cerberus, and the staff as the toiling cleaners of the Styx. There is something fateful about the figure of the manager and his irritating and irate orders.

> "....decency? Where are the decent people... Where will you find people like that? Why on earth does this wretched curtain have to be torn to shreds... and why hasn't this damn blind been mended?
> ...Riffraff, ragamuffins and scum are tearing the place down!"

And he continues issuing his orders:

> "We can take used candles and light them just before they come in... The brawn and beetroot and Italian salad... out! And three carnations in each vase will be enough... What do they expect for thirty kronor, the bloody swine!
>
> These funerals... they're enough to kill you."

When Giliap has been introduced into this suffocating environment he simply puts on his waiter's jacket and starts work. The funeral party arrives. In the same way as in the crayfish party in *A Swedish Love Story* during the ceremony that follows Andersson takes the opportunity to study and expose attitudes and behaviour. The funeral guests have only had a short time to adapt to their roles as mourners, but in varying degrees they are given the opportunity and the scope to give vent to their grief. Many of them seize the chance to give free rein to the feelings of which they are deprived by the officious laws of everyday life.

This prelude is very effective, since *Giliap* is a story about people without any relation to their feelings. The whole film is set at a lethargic tempo. The characters are fettered by hesitation and lack of enterprise. Since they are not sure who they are, they have no ability to express themselves, either verbally or emotionally. Andersson therefore seeks to convey "what they're like," visual impressions, their presence, movements, nerve vibrations. Time seems to have stopped. The characters appear to be puppets, ruled by an ineluctable fate. Something is happening to them, something which seems to lie beyond their control. The eerily delayed pace of the film endows the drama with an almost hallucinatory effect.

One dramatic idea put into effect with great thoroughness is that the different characters should always be regarded by someone. The observer changes, but the characters in a scene always have their relations in space and to each other defined by an outsider who is a witness to their goings-on. This contributes to the sense of claustrophobia which exists even in the most spacious and open of *Giliap's* indoor settings. It creates a feeling of indignation in the spectator. One feels a desire to grab hold of these people and shake them out of their passivity and get them to act on the strength of their inherent but suffocated resources of life and passion.

The Count bases his course of action on this paralysis. He involves Giliap in his plans, just as he earlier sought allies among the other fugitives at the hotel. And Giliap allows himself to be persuaded by the Count's promises and claims, despite the fact that doubt is crying out from behind his impassive features.

But the Count is poorly equipped for his big *coup*. He has bolstered up his self-esteem and

Thommy Berggren and Mona Seilitz in GILIAP

forged his plans in the isolation afforded by the protective walls of the hotel. He becomes a victim of his dreams, and the plan fails miserably.

Giliap is about things that have been lost. Roy Andersson has stated that *Giliap* is about "a feeling in our time." This is neither a simplified nor a cryptic statement. Andersson senses that for many people life is not enough, that many people are going around with the feeling that they and

their lives have been robbed of something essential, a quality of life that the society in which we live is in the process of killing off. This lost something is what Giliap and Andersson are trying to get closer to.

Giliap is a provocative film. By its objectivity it invites the observer to enter into the picture. But the reflective rhythm and utterly dispassionate presentation of the fortunes of its characters give rise to a sense of indignation. We are unable to enter the images to influence or to act. We are forced to become accomplices to the paralysis of the characters.

The leading part in *Giliap* must have presented Thommy Berggren with a challenge. Berggren is almost completely dumb in the film. He gives a portrait of a vague, taciturn and unfulfilled man who guides his life with a sort of honesty and emotional rationality. Giliap is certainly a lodestone for the audience, but the role itself lacks an identity, expressing stark passivity. Thommy Berggren is, of course, an actor with a strong stage presence and powers of expression, but here he is made to act in a more subdued and non-committal style than we associate with him. Andersson seems to have operated on similar principles in choosing Anita Lindblom to play the neurotically disturbed aunt in *A Swedish Love Story*. He went against her conventional image, and Anita Lindblom responded to the challenge by giving a superbly gripping character study. Similarly, Thommy Berggren creates a convincing and almost trans-lucent portrait of bewilderment and hypersensitivity. In Thommy Berggren's interpretation Giliap is a very compound and contradictory character, in the tension between a heart-felt emotion and expressions of will and passions which are completely shackled.

The film's strong suggestiveness is strengthened by the elements of myth and mysticism draped around the keenly observed realistic events. There is a tremendous sharpness of detail on all levels. The *décor* contributes to the creation of a kind of enhanced realism. The actors are aided by real-life professionals, waiters, cooks and kitchen staff. *Giliap* does indeed strive to be "one step above everyday life," but reality is the starting point. The film elucidates and refines it. The images are concentrated and expressive. The camera moves decisively, and with the aid of the lighting produces a painting charged with emotion which sensualises our experience.

In *Giliap* Roy Andersson has created a poem. In this poem there are no statues. There are characters embodying the dilemmas, the alienation, the absence which are indisputably and relentlessly symptomatic of this life of ours.

11 The Three-Dimensional Man

In the late Sixteenth Century the Spanish physician Juan Huarte published a study on the nature of human intelligence. He observed that the word for intelligence, *ingenio,* has the same Latin root as various words meaning "engender" or "generate." This, he argued, gave a clue to the nature of mind.

In his linguistic study on language and mind Noam Chomsky quotes Huarte as distinguishing three levels of intelligence. The lowest of these is the "docile wit". The next highest level, normal human intelligence, is able to "engender within itself, by its own power, the principles on which knowledge rests." Normal human minds are such that "assisted by the subject alone, without the help of anybody, they will produce a thousand conceits they never heard spoke of... inventing and saying such things as they never heard from their masters, nor any mouth." Normal human intelligence is capable of acquiring knowledge through its own internal resources; it is capable of generating new thoughts and of finding appropriate and novel ways of expressing them, in ways that entirely transcend any training or experience.

Huarte maintains that the difference between docile wit and normal intelligence, with its full generative capacities, is the distinction between beast and man.

Huarte postulates a third kind of wit, "by means of which some, without art or study, speak such subtle and surprising things, yet true, that were never before seen, heard or writ, no, nor ever so much as thought of." The reference here is to true creativity, an exercise of the creative imagination in ways that go beyond normal intelligence and may involve a "mixture of madness."

Lasse Forsberg confronts us with a representative of this kind of creative intelligence in his film *The Assault. The Assault* is a series of confrontations and provocations which formulate a number of impatient questions. And the answers are pessimistic, since society reacts repressively. It responds with resistance, unleashing defence mechanisms whose function is to stupefy and kill. Empirical science and the system of "normal" reactions and conditions which society is so anxious to safeguard are unable to accept the power of the creative impulses which the main character in the film emits. His surprise attacks on a system of knowledge so careful to mark out its boundaries must be quelled. His antagonistic behaviour and ideas are labelled with suitable diagnostic terms from medicine: schizophrenia, pathological. Anyone who diverges is taken into care for re-adjustment to the "normality" which he is resisting.

Poets and artists still go free. For the time being their imaginations still have a commercial value. But those who do not use paper or easel, living their poetic sense of reality in real life, are led away to silent, locked rooms to be drugged into uniformity and indifference.

* * *

"Look at this lot, eh! You know, when you come to think... What a bloody crime against these people! Look! There they go like, like, like little performing robots. What for? WHAT FOR?!

"Eh, look at that coat down there! And that coat there, and that coat there! Do you know what it is? It's systematic indoctrination of human material to get them to consume! And what's behind it all? Why the hell can't they make jackets, shoes, hats, caps and cars that'll last for five or ten years? They're not allowed to. Do you realise that they produce a jacket today which is ready for the rubbish-tip tomorrow just so that a few capitalists can sit making money all the time. Do you realise that this is systematic indoctrination and destruction of human material. What a tragedy! Imagine what qualities these people have inside themselves if they could be emancipated and liberated from exploitation by this economic mechanism!

"Look at them, look at them obediently walking along! See? Well brought-up, decent people. Every Sunday they sit at home eating their cake and watching their telly. Every Tuesday they go out and get thumped in the head, systematically, by everything that needs buying. Look at this advertising all around you! Buy, buy this, buy that, buy the other, buy the lot... Buy this, buy that... Systematic exploitation!

"It's a crime! They're criminals for Christ's sake! We live in a criminal society! That's why I say that the ones who are the criminals in this society are actually the ones who are protesting against this criminality... That's why the criminals are basically the honest ones, and the honest ones are the criminals...

"They have to be robots so that a bloody upper class can profiteer out of them. Have you ever thought about that?

'Man's recorded history is five thousand years old. But more has happened in the last fifty years than in all the others put together. Mankind is half a million years old, but more has happened in the last fifty years...

'What's going to happen in the next two hundred years? Perhaps man is in the process of evolving into something entirely new and becoming an entirely new being. The new race will be the non-aggressive man. And what is it that's obstructing this social development? Well, it's the social structure we live under. The upper class pushing down the lower class. Pushing them down into illiteracy, pushing them down into poverty, pushing them down into starvation, wasting and throwing away the potential human intelligences which could be put to some useful purpose. The cork... That damn cork blocking all development. If only it would vanish... If only the cork vanished, mankind would undergo a technical and social explosion. If only the cork would vanish..."

Knut Nielsen, the main character in *The Assault,* is standing on a viaduct with his friend Björn observing the people passing beneath him, the well-adjusted and the adaptable, hurrying past through the city. Knut regards them as test-tube babies shut up in a stultifying aquarium existence. None of them seems to have tried to tap his innate and highly personal qualities and ambitions. Knut wants to ease out the cork and set free all the thoughts, emotions and dreams which are now forced to recede into the background in the face of demands which he feels to be false and inimical to human nature. He wishes to see a development releasing the resources of mankind, a liberation process which is not stopped short by the narrow, egoistic profitability considerations of capitalist society.

Knut is forever at war, in opposition. He does not seek opportunities for giving scope to his views. He creates them. He frequently comes into conflict with the people he meets. They defend themselves against his aggressive volubility, his

Knut Pettersen with his friend on the viaduct in THE ASSAULT

smooth yet nagging persuasiveness.

One day Knut comes face to face with one of these well adjusted social climbers and he seizes the opportunity of giving his views an airing. The man — who might be a company director in early middle-age — is standing alongside his Jaguar when he is "attacked" by Knut's indignant stream of words. Knut sees the man as a living example of what he calls the "cork" in society, the cork obstructing all efforts to attain equality. The man exploits and lives well off the labour of the productive forces in society. His Jaguar is the symbol of exploitation: "...Do you know who produced this Jaguar? Do you know who the productive factors are in society that make it possible for you to drive around in a Jaguar at all? Have you ever thought about it? Have you ever thought that those who keep this society going, producing goods which you consume — your bloody coat, here, your bloody Jaguar — are a result of production. And the distribution of this production result is that you can ride around in a Jag costing fifty thousand! Who produced that Jag? The workers produced your bloody Jag. It's MY Jag you're driving!"

The man refuses to engage in any kind of discussion. When he turns away, and Knut notices that his arguments are incapable of making any impression, he responds with an aggressiveness stemming from despair. He punches the man on the jaw. That ought to be an argument he can grasp, anyway!

Charges are brought against Knut for assault, and he is arraigned before the officials of the legal machinery: police interrogators, personal investigators, psychologists, and finally the staff of a

Knut argues with the psychiatrist

mental hospital. Their verdict is unanimous. Knut is sick and should be isolated from society. He is sentenced to psychiatric treatment in confinement.

The Assault is built up through a series of monologues and conversations in which Knut tries in various ways to express his views on life and his experiences of it. With his almost desperate faith in himself and his ideas, Knut is the driving force in these confrontations. He is convincing in his analyses, firm in his faith in the justice which he feels to be absolute. Yet in spite of this he emerges as a victim. And he also becomes the loser who is sacrificed for the sake of outward peace and tranquillity. The final diagnosis is a triumph for the pharmaceutical industry: 3 x 75 klorpronoxen, 50 nozarin and tofranil, in gradually increasing doses. . .

Knut's tragedy is that nobody speaks the same language as he does. The man with the Jaguar whom he provokes dare not answer his case, nor has he any arguments with which to do so. The interrogators and investigators have no personal vocabulary extending beyond the blunt questions necessary for the record. The doctors and hospital staff have neither the time nor the interest to approach Knut on a human level. They resort to ever heavier sedation or, when they find the patient excessively troublesome, to violence. They strap him down to the hospital bed. There the film leaves Knut.

What is particularly tragic in Knut's case is that not even those close to him are able to understand or even come anywhere near to sharing his way of giving vent to his social protest. Knut regards his friend, the actor Björn, as someone who has appropriated his socialist views without making contact with them deep down inside. They are simply a veneer. Knut accuses Björn of being a "leftwing Nazi," a *petit bourgeois* who finds it romantic and trendy to be revolutionary; for whom the socialist revolution is only a compensation, a compensatory protest against an authoritarian upbringing and an authoritarian father.

It is easy to see Knut as an arrogant character, superior and self-righteous both in his attacks on the powers-that-be and on those he considers his friends. But anyone who does not see and experience the despair underlying Knut's onslaughts is opting to see only a part of the creative force which Knut actually is. Like other creative people, Knut lives in profound insecurity and isolation. His actions are an attempt to break out of this isolation.

Lasse Forsberg's film does not present Knut Nielsen as a consistently appealing person. But who would demand such a thing, either of Forsberg or of Knut? Knut says that he dreams of the aggressionless society. Yet what are we living in? We lead a life in which aggressions are regarded with horror and suspicion. Aggressions must be broken down and subdued, whether this is to be done by soothing persuasion or the appropriate doses of psycho-pharmaceutical drugs. In this way they are ostracised, those who seek our attention and support for their ideas. They receive neither an answer nor any positive resistance. They are left alone with their despair, abandoned.

Forsberg conducts his discussion on many levels. He not only shows us Knut's dilemma but also Björn's, the "romantic revolutionary" who takes the girl from the dry cleaner's home with him to convert her to the true socialist faith. But his "educational" ambitions do not stretch any further than their relationship. He lets the baby out with the bath-water, so to speak. The socialist ideas form a merely decorative feature of the seduction.

Forsberg also confronts Björn with the professional writer on culture, living comfortably off his radical commitment, for whom the veneer affects his wallet and human interest comes a poor second. This is a very effective ironic scene, with the journalist absent-mindedly listening to his visitor and asking him to do things for him while he hammers away at his article on the situation of the low-paid workers.

The Assault is a debate of ideas which is intelligently formulated on all levels. It is executed with more awareness than all the socially orientated and more documentary descriptions of the present which were an encouraging reality in the late Sixties. The film was a collective effort, the participants joining the project on equal terms. The director is responsible for the basic framework of the film, and the actors (mostly from the free theatre group "Narren") contribute their own lines and arguments. The vitality of the film stems above all from Knut Pettersen's intense and intelligent acting in the main role. He lays bare emotions and thoughts, and his powerful, self-revealing acting is full of compulsion.

Knut is led away, isolated and locked up. He is already lost. His punishment, aiming at re-adjustment, can never result in anything except the disintegration of the positive forces within him.

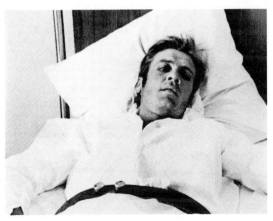

Knut is strapped to the hospital bed

Isolation mutilates the intelligence. The mind is only capable of receiving stimuli through the senses and associating them with one another and with the memory. Without impulses from outside, without ideas and thoughts allowing the develop-ment of knowledge and the ability to think, human creativity dies.

In this respect *The Assault* serves as a warning signal and a speech for the defence. It may be hard for us to accept Knut and his embarrassing honesty. But he is entitled to demand that we make the effort.

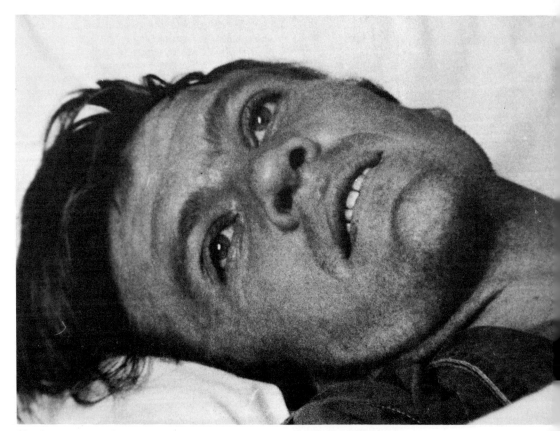

The last close-up of Knut in THE ASSAULT

Filmographies

Bo Widerberg

Born 8 June 1930 in Malmö. Has a working-class background. Finished school at the age of seventeen. Made his *début* as an author in 1952 with the novel "Hösttermin" and the short-story collection "Kyssas." Has also written the novels "På botten av himlen" (1954), "Erotikon" (1957) and "Den gröna draken" (1959), as well as the short-story collection "Kejsaren av Capri" (1955). Has also written stage plays. In 1962 he published the polemic book "The Vision in Swedish Film." Has worked as a stage director at (Stadsteatern) The Public Theatre of Stockholm and (Dramaten) The Dramatic Theatre of Stockholm. Acted in Palle Kjaerulff-Schmidt's picture "The Story of Barbara."

Short Films

POJKEN OCH DRAKEN (The Boy and the Dragon)
p — Bo Widerberg 1961. *sc* — Bo Widerberg. *ph* — Jan Troell. *m* — Vivaldi. *ed* — Bo Widerberg, Jan Troell. l.p. — Arild Möller *Boy,* Bodil Mathiasson, Ulla-Greta Starck, Rune Turesson. 20 mins.

TVÅBARNSMOR, VÄNTANDE HENNES TREDJE (Mother of Two, Pregnant with Her Third)
p — Bo Widerberg, 1970. *sc* — Bo Widerberg. *ph* — Bo Widerberg, Peter Schildt. *ed* — Bo Widerberg. *l.p* — Vanessa Redgrave.

Feature Films

BARNVAGNEN (The Pram/The Baby-Carriage)
p — Gustav Scheutz. *p.c* — Europa Film 1962. *sc* — Bo Widerberg. *ph* — Jan Torell. *m* — Jan Johansson. *sd* — Sven Rydh. *ed* — Wic' Kjellin. *l.p* — Inger Taube *Britt,* Thommy Berggren *Björn,* Lars Passgård *Robban,* Ulla Akselsson *Britt's Mother,* Gunnar Öhlund *Britt's Father,* Bill Jönsson *Britt's Younger Brother,* Stig Torstensson *The Boy On the Stairs,* Lena Brundin *Britt's Friend,* Nina Widerberg *The Neighbours' Daughter.* 95 mins.

KVARTERET KORPEN (Raven's End)
p — Gustav Scheutz. *p.c* —Europa Film 1963. *sc* — Bo Widerberg. *ph* — Jan Lindeström. *sd* — Sven Fahlén. *m* — Vivaldi. *ed* — Wic' Kjellin. *a.d.* — Einar Nettelbladt. *l.p* — Thommy Berggren *Anders,* Keve Hjelm *His Father,* Emy Storm *His Mother,* Ingvar Hirdwall *Sixten,* Christina Frambäck *Elsie,* Agneta Prytz *The Woman Next-door,* Nina Widerberg *The Girl with the Glasses.* 100 mins.

KÄRLEK 65 (Love 65)
p — Gustav Scheutz. *p.c* — Europa Film 1965. *sc* — Bo Widerberg. *ph* — Jan Lindeström. *sd* — Sven Fahlén. *m*— Vivaldi. *ed* — Bo Widerberg. *l.p.* — Keve Hjelm *Keve,* Ann-Marie Gyllenspetz *Ann-Marie,* Inger Taube *Inger,* Evabritt Strandberg *Evabritt,* Ben Carruthers *Himself,* Björn *Gustafsson* Björn, Kent Andersson *Kent,* Nina Widerberg *Nina,* Thommy Berggren, Agneta Ekmanner *The actors.* 96 mins.

HEJA ROLAND! (Thirty Times Your Money)
p.c — Europa Film 1966. *sc* — Bo Widerberg, from his own novel "The Green Dragon." *ph* — Jörgen Persson. *sd* — Lars Klettner. *ed* — Bo Widerberg. *l.p* — Thommy Berggren *Roland Jung,* Mona Malm *Nanna Jung,* Ulf Palme *ÖJ,* Holger Löwenadler *W. Vassén,* Madeleine Sundgren *Britt Lennert,* Carl Billqvist *Svensson,* Lars-Göran Carlsson *Mortell,* Ingvar Kjellson *Skog, Cashier,* Eddie Axberg *Sten Hansson,* Catharina Edfeldt *A Girl in Her Teens.* 96 mins.

ELVIRA MADIGAN
p.c — Europa Film 1967. *sc* — Bo Widerberg. *ph* — Jörgen Persson (Eastmancolor). *sd* — Sven Fahlén. *m*— Mozart's Piano Concerto No. 21. *ed* — Bo Widerberg. *l.p* — Pia Degermark *Elvira Madigan,* Thommy Berggren *Sixten Sparre,* Lennart Malmer *Sixten's Friend,* Cleo *The Cook,* Nina Widerberg *The Girl.* 91 mins.

DEN VITA SPORTEN (The White Game)
p — Grupp 13. *p.c* — Svenska Filminstitutet/Svensk Filmindustri 1969. *Grupp 13:* Roy Andersson, Kalle Boman, Lena Ewert, Sven Fahlén, Staffan Hedqvist, Axel Lohman, Lennart Malmer, Jörgen Persson, Ingela Romare, Inge Roos, Rudi Spee, Bo Widerberg, Björn Öberg. 100 mins.

ÅDALEN 31 (The Ådalen Riots)

p.c —Svensk Filmindustri 1969. sc — Bo Widerberg. ph Jörgen Persson (Eastmancolor, Techniscope). sd — Björn Öberg. m— The Internationale, Chopin. ed — Bo Widerberg. l.p — Peter Schildt Kjell, Kerstin Tidelius His Mother, Roland Hedlund His Father, Stefan Feierbach Åke, Martin Widerberg Martin, Marie De Geer Anna, Anita Björk The Manager's Wife, Olof Bergström Manager, Jonas Bergström Nisse, Olle Björling A Strike-breaker, Pierre Lindstedt The Foreman. 113 mins.

JOE HILL (The Ballad of Joe Hill)

p.c. — Bo Widerberg Film 1971 sc — Bo Widerberg. ph — Petter Davidsson, Jörgen Persson (Eastmancolor). sd — Ulf Darin, Lars-Erik Ulander. m — Stefan Grossman. a.d — Ulf Axén. ed — Bo Widerberg. l.p. — Thommy Berggren Joe Hill, Anja Schmidt Lucia, Kelvin Malave "Räven" (The Fox), Evert Andersson Blackie, Cathy Smith Cathy, Hasse Persson Paul, David Moritz David, Richard Weber Richard, Joel Miller Ed Rowan, Robert Faeder George, Wendy Geier Elisabeth Gurley Flynn, Franco Molinari The Tenor, Liska March The Sister of Mercy. 115 mins.

FIMPEN (Stubby)

p.c — Bo Widerberg Film 1974. sc — Bo Widerberg. ph — John Olsson, Hanno Fuchs, Roland Sterner, Åke Astrand (Eastmancolor, Techniscope). sd —Ulf Reinhard, Christer Furubrand, Jan Brodin. m — Sergej Prokofiev. ed — Bo Widerberg. l.p — Johan Bergman "Stubby", Monica Zetterlund The Teacher, Magnus Härenstam "Mackan," Ernst-Hugo Järegård The Club Captain, Carl Billquist The Headmaster, Stig Ossian Ericson Taxi-driver, Inger Bergman "Stubby's Mother, Arne Bergman Stubby's father, Annelie Bergman Stubby's sister and Georg "Åby" Ericson and the Swedish National Team. 89 mins.

VILGOT SJÖMAN

Born 2 December 1924 in Stockholm. Student-theatre during his school days. Acts, directs and writes plays. Made his début as an novelist 1948 with "Lektorn" (The Teacher). Since then has published "Kvinnobild" 1952, "Flygblad" 1956 "Lek på regnbågen" 1958, "I Hollywood" 1961, "Hollywood flyger till Pentagon" 1961, "L 136, dagbok med Ingmar Bergman" 1963, "Jag var nyfiken, dagbok med mig själv" 1967, "Lisel, en medaljong" 1968, "Surdegen" 1969. Has written and directed for the stage "Hattasken" 1964 and "Pojken i sängen" 1969, and some plays that remain unperformed. Has written the film scripts Trots (from his own novel "The Teacher", dir. Gustaf Molander), Lek på regnbågen (1952, dir. Lars-Eric Kjellgren) and Siska (1958, dir. Alf Kjellin). Been active with literary, theatre and film criticism. Has made interview programs and short films for TV. Has acted in Ingmar Bergman's The Shame and in some of his own films.

Short Films

NEGRESSEN I SKÅPET (The Negress in the Cupboard)

p.c — Svensk Filmindustri 1966. sc — Vilgot Sjöman. ph — Rune Ericson. sd — Olof Unnerstad. s.d — Rolf Boman. ed — C.O. Skeppstedt. l.p — Glenna Foster Jones The Negress, Lars Ekborg The Husband, Inga Landgré The Wife.

RESA MED FAR (Journey with Father)

p — Vilgot Sjöman 1968. sc — Vilgot Sjöman. ph — Olle Ohlsson. ed — Peter Billing. l.p — Wiktor Sjöman, Vilgot Sjöman.

BRÖDERNA KARLSSON (The Karlsson Brothers)

p — Vilgot Sjöman, Filmstugan 1971. sc — Vilgot Sjöman ph —Rune Ericson. ed — C.O. Skeppstedt. l.p — Wiktor Sjöman and the four Karlsson brothers. 20 mins.

ÄLSKADE JEANETTE MACDONALD (My Beloved Jeanette MacDonald)

p — Vilgot Sjöman/Filmstugan 1971. sc — Vilgot Sjöman. ph — Rune Ericson.

Feature Films

ÄLSKARINNAN (The Mistress)

p.c — Svensk Filmindustri 1962. p — Allan Ekelund. sc — Vilgot Sjöman. ph —Lars Björne (CinemaScope). sd — Stig Flodin. ed — Lennart Wallén. a.d — P.A. Lundgren. l.p — Bibi Andersson The Girl, Per Myrberg The Boy, Max von Sydow The Man, Öllegård Wellton The Man's Wife, Birgitta Valberg Motherly Woman, Gunnar Olsson The Old Man. Birger Lensander The Sleeping-car Conductor. 80 mins.

p.c — Svensk Filmindustri. *p* — Allan Ekelund. *sc* — Lars Görling, from his own novel. *ph* — Gunnar Fischer. *sd* — P.O. Petterson. *m* — Georg Riedel. *a.d* — P.A. Lundgren. *ed* — Lennart Wallén. *l.p* — Lars Lind *Krister,* Leif Nymark *Nisse,* Stig Törnblom *Egon,* Lars Hansson *Pyret,* Sven Algotsson *Jingis,* Torleif Cederstrand *Slaktarn,* Bo Andersson Fisken (*the "Fish"*), Lena Nyman *Steva,* Frank Sundström *The Inspector,* Åke Grönberg *Reverend Mild,* Mona Andersson *Kajsa,* Siegfrid Wald, Wilhelm Fricke *German sailors,* Erik Hell, Leif Liljeroth *Policemen,* Jan Blomberg. 99 mins.

KLÄNNINGEN (The Dress)

p.c — Svensk Filmindustri 1963. *sc* — Ulla Isaksson. *ph* — Sven Nykvist. *sd* — Brian Wikström. *m* — Erik Nordgren. *a.d* — Bibi Lindström. *ed* — Ulla Ryghe. *l.p* — Gunn Wallgren *Helen Fürst,* Gunnar Björnstrand *Helmer Berg,* Tina Hedström *Edit Fürst,* Mimi Pollack *Mrs. Rubin,* Conny Borg *Young Man,* Ellika Mann, Fillie Lyckow, Berit Tancred *Saleswomen,* Lars Berenett *Errand-boy.* 85 mins.

SYSKONBÄDD (My Sister, My Love)

p.c — Sandrews 1965. *p* — Göran Lindgren. *sc* — Vilgot Sjöman. *ph* — Lars Björne. *sd* — Tage Sjöborg. *a.d* — P.A. Lundgren. *ed* — Lennart Wallén, Wic'Kjellin. *l.p* — Jarl Kulle *Baron Alsmeden,* Bibi Andersson *Charlotte,* Per Oscarsson *Jacob,* Gunnar Björnstrand *Count Schwartz,* Tina Hedström *Ebba Livin,* Berta Hall *Mrs. Küller, The Old Woman,* Åke Lindström *Her Son,* Kjerstin Dellert *Mrs. Olin,* Lena Hansson *Blonde Woman,* Thomas Ungwitter *Her Husband,* Gudrun Östbye *Dressmaker,* Lasse Pöysti *Visitor at the Tavern,* Chris Wahlström *Tavern Hostess.* 96 mins.

JAG ÄR NYFIKEN — GUL (I Am Curious — Yellow)

p.c — Sandrews 1966-67. *p* — Göran Lindgren. *sc* — Vilgot Sjöman. *ph* — Peter Wester. *sd* — Tage Sjöborg. *m* — Bengt Ernryd. *ed* — Wic'Kjellin. *l.p* — Lena Nyman *Lena,* Börje Ahlstedt *Börje,* Peter Lindgren *Lena's Father,* Chris Wahlström *His Woman,* Magnus Nilsson *Magnus,* Marie Göranzon *Börje's Wife,* Ulla Lyttkens *Lena's Friend,* Holger Löwenadler *The King,* Börje Ahlstedt *Crown Prince,* Hans Hellberg *Lena's ex-lover.* Bim Warne *Bim,* Martin Luther King, Yevgeni Yevtushenko, Olof Palme, Vilgot Sjöman *Themselves.* 121 mins.

JAG ÄR NYFIKEN — BLÅ (I Am Curious — Blue)

p.c — Sandrews 1966-67. *p* — Göran Lindgren. *sc* Vilgot Sjöman. *ph* — Peter Wester. *sd* — Tage Sjöborg, Thomas Holewa. *m* — Bengt Ernryd, Bengt Palmers. *ed* — Wic'Kjellin. *l.p* — Lena Nyman *Lena,* Börje Ahlstedt *Börje,* Peter Lindgren *Lena's Father,* Gudrun Östbye *Lena's Mother,* Sonja Lindgren *Girl in the Shop,* Gunnel Broström *Woman on the Island,* Hanne Sandemose *Her Friend,* Frej Lindqvist *Friend's Husband,* Marie Göranzon *Börje's Wife,* Bertil Wikström *Doctor,* Vilgot Sjöman *Himself.* 107 mins.

NI LJUGER (You're Lying)

p.c — Sandrews 1969. *p* Göran Lindgren. *sc* — Vilgot Sjöman from a novel of Lars Karlsson and Björn Vilson. *ph* — Olle Ohlsson. *sd* — Gunnar Nilsson. *m* Ulf Björlin, Cornelis Vreeswijk. *a.d* — Charles Delattre. *ed* — C. O. Skeppstedt. *l.p* — Stig Engström *Lasse,* Börje Ahlstedt *Björn,* Sif Ruud *Anna, Björn's Mother,* Anita Ekström *Margot,* Rune Turesson *John,* Barbro Nordin *Lasse's Hostess,* Olof Bergström *Chairman of the Institution-committee,* Torsten Lilliecrona *Inspector of Prison Discipline,* Jan-Erik Lindqvist *Psychiatrist,* Sture Ericsson *Prison Doctor.* 107 mins.

LYCKLIGA SKITAR (Blushing Charlie)

p.c — Sandrews 1970. *p* — Göran Lindgren. *sc* — Vilgot Sjöman, Bernt Lundqvist, Solveig Ternström. *ph* — Rune Ericson (Eastmancolor, Super 16). *sd* — Ulf Darin. *m* — Lasse Werner and His Friends. *a.d* — Charles Delattre. *ed* — C.O. Skeppstedt. *l.p* — Bernt Lundquist *Charlie,* Solveig Ternström *Pia,* Tomas Bolme *PV,* Inger Liljefors *Anita,* Christer Boustedt *Krille,* Lasse Werner *Lasse,* Gösta Wälivaara *Gösta,* Janne Carlsson *Janne,* Bertil Norström *Hansson, Charlie's Boss,* Olle Andersson *Accountant,* Janet Pettersson *"Taxen,"* Lilian Johansson *"Ärtan,"* the *Bunny-Girl.* 96 mins.

TROLL (Trolls/Till Sex Do Us Part)

p — Vilgot Sjöman/Filmstugan 1971. *sc* — Vilgot Sjöman, Solveig Ternström, Börje Ahlstedt, Margaretha Byström, Frej Lindqvist. *ph* — Rune Ericson (Eastmancolor, Super 16) *sd* — Ulf Darin. *ed* — C.O. Skeppstedt. *l.p* — Solveig Ternström *Maja,* Börje Ahlstedt *Rikard,* Margaretha Byström *Lillemor,* Frej Lindqvist *Sture,* Jan-Olof Strandberg *Priest,* Sven Björling, Gösta Bredefeldt *Workers at the Crematorium,* Akke Carlsson *Worker,* Nina Gaines *Nurse,* Vilgot Sjöman *Doctor,* Barbro Ericsson, Ingegärd Käll, Rolf Björling, Hans Johansson, Rolf Jupiter *Opera-singers.* 99 mins.

EN HANDFULL KARLEK (A Handful of Love)

p.c — Svenska Filminstitutet/Sandrews 1973. *p* — Bengt Forslund. *sc* — Vilgot Sjöman. *ph* — Jörgen Persson (Eastmancolor). *sd* — Tomas Samuelsson, Lennart Forssén. *m* Bengt Ernryd. *a.d* — P.A. Lundgren. *ed* — Wic'Kjellin. *l.p* — Anita Ekström *Hjördis,* Gösta Bredefeldt *Daniel Severin Larsson,* Ingrid Thulin *Inez Crona,* Ernst Hugo Järegård *Claes Crona,* Evabritt Strandberg *Thérèse,* Sif Ruud *Thekla Rehnholm,* Per Myrberg *Sebastian Rehnholm,* Frej Lindqvist *Fritz Fredrik Crona,* Ernst Günther *Theodor Litz, "Finland,"* Gunnar Ossiander *Grandfather Crona,* Anders Oscarsson *Henning Christian Crona,* Chris Wahlström *Magdalena, the Cook,* Bibi Skoglund *Adèle, the Maid,* Claire Wikholm *Zaida, the Nanny,* Harald Hamrell *Linus, Hjördis's Younger Brother,* Lise-Lotte Nilsson *Hanna, Hjördis's Sister,* Rolf Skoglund *Sigfrid,* Bellan Ross *Grandmother,* Berndt Lundquist *Karl Inge Svensson,* Jan-Erik Lindqvist *Ivan Persson,* Pierre Lindstedt *Nicklasson,* Georg Rydeberg Director *Apelberg.* 142 mins.

GARAGET (The Garage)

p.c — Europa Film/Public Commercial Produktion 1975. *sc* — Vilgot Sjöman. *ph* — Petter Davidsson (Eastmancolor). *sd* —Thomas Holéwa. *ed* — Wic'Kjellin. *l.p* — Agneta Edmanner *Pia,* Frej Lindqvist *Andreas,* Christina Schollin *Nancy,* Per Myrberg *Ulf,* Lil Terselius *Gun,* Peter Lindgren *Adolphson,* Kerstin Hanström *Sylvia,* Annika Tretow *Mrs. Ohlsson,* Axel Düberg *Mr. Ohlsson,* Carl Billquist *Doctor,* Annika Levin *School-girl,* Åke Fridell *Siste Baron ("Last Lord"),* Mona Andersson *Hairdresser,* Rolf Skoglund *Guy at Filling Station,* Evert Granholm *Master Ståhl.*

KJELL GREDE

Born 12 August 1936 in Stockholm. After taking his degrees at the University of Stockholm he worked as a teacher. Active as a journalist, author and painter.

Member of the government committee investigating film in Sweden, and since 1973 manager of The Swedish Film Institute's Workshop. Directed a TV serial based on Strindberg's "A Madman's Defence" in 1975.

Short Film

SOTAREN (The Chimney-Sweep)

p.c — Sandrews 1966. *p* — Bo Jonsson. *sc* — Kjell Grede. *ph* — Rune Ericson. *ed* — Lars Hagström. *l.p* — Jan-Olof Strandberg *Chimney-Sweep,* Lis Nilheim *Girl at the Window.*

Feature Films

HUGO OCH JOSEFIN (Hugo and Josefin)

p.c — Sandrews 1967. *p* - Göran Lindgren. *sc* — Maria Gripe, Kjell Grede, from Maria Gripe's children's books. *ph* — Lars Björne (Eastmancolor). *sd* — Lennart Engholm. *m* — Torbjörn Lundquist. *ed* — Lars Hagström. *l.p* — Fredrik Becklén *Hugo,* Marie Öhman *Josefin,* Inga Landgré *Josefin's Mother,* Helena Brodin *Teacher,* Bellan Roos *Lyra,* Beppe Wolgers *Gudmarsson, the Gardener.* 81 mins.

HARRY MUNTER (Harry Munter)

p.c — Sandrews 1969. *p* — Göran Lindgren. *sc* — Kjell Grede. *ph* — Lars Björne (Eastmancolor). *sd* — Bengt Kåring. *m* — Johann Strauss. *ed* — Lars Hagström. *l.p* — Jan Nielsen *Harry Munter,* Carl-Gustaf Lindstedt *Valle,* Gun Jönsson *Gudrun,* George Adelly *Manne,* Al Simon *The American,* Elina Salo *Lonely Woman,* Inga Dahlbeck *Girl No. 1,* Britt-Marie Engström *Girl No. 2,* Paul Westerlund *Grim,* Gerda Calander *Kristina Birgitta Eleonor,* Märta Allan-Jonson *Grandmother.* 101 mins.

KLARA LUST

p.c — Sandrews 1971. *p* Göran Lindgren. *sc* — Kjell Grede. *ph* — Lars Björne (Eastmancolor). *sd* — Bengt Kåring. *m* — Gustav Mahler, Symphony No. 7. *ed* — Lars Hagström. *l.p* — Lars Brännström *Helge,* Gunilla Olsson *Klara Lust,* Carl-Gustaf Lindstedt *The Mighty Man,* Agneta Prytz *The Mother,* Ulla-Britt Norrman *Murva,* Harald Merseburg *Grim,* Conny Larsson *"Klokdåren" (The Mad-Wise),* Carl-Olof Alm *Lover,* Gösta Prüzelius *Father,* Elisabeth Grönqvist *Naked Girl with the Soup,* Mari Isedal *Owner of the Kiosk.* 103 mins.

EN ENKEL MELODI (A Simple Melody)

p.c — Sandrews 1974. *p* — Göran Lindgren. *sc* — Kjell

Grede. *ph* — Lars Björne (Eastmancolor). *sd* — Tommy Sundqvist. *m* — Björn J:son Lindh, Johann Strauss's "Emperor Waltz." *ed* — Wic'Kjellin, Lars Hagström. *l.p* — Kjell Bergqvist *Felix Jonsson*, Maj-Britt Nilsson *Mother*, Ulf Johansson *Father*, Ingmari Johansson *Girl*, Gösta Bernhard *Doctor*, Eddie Axberg *Hugo*, Lena Hansson *Margareta*, Kent Andersson *Doctor*, Stig Ossian Ericson *Farmer*, Kim Anderzon *Doctor's Mistress*, Tord Peterson, Galizia Renza. 98 mins.

JAN TROELL

Born 23 July 1931 in Malmö. After finishing school he became a teacher. His interest in photography began early and at the end of the Fifties he began making instructional films for children. Besides shooting his own films, he photographed Widerberg's first feature film, *The Pram*. Has directed one TV play.

Short Films

STAD (Town)
p — Jan Troell 1959. *sc* — Jan Troell. *ph* — Jan Troell. *ed* — Jan Troell.

SOMMARTÅG
p — Jan Troell 1960. *sc* Jan Troell. *ph* — Jan Troell. *ed* — Jan Troell. 13 mins.

POJKEN OCH DRAKEN (The Boy and the Dragon)
p — Bo Widerberg, Jan Troell 1961. *sc* — Bo Widerberg. *d* — Bo Widerberg. *ph* — Jan Troell. *l.p* — Arild Möller *Boy*, Bodil Mathiasson, Ulla-Greta Starck, Rune Turesson. 20 mins.

BÅTEN (The Boat)
p — Jan Troell 1962. *sc* — Jan Troell. *ph* — Jan Troell (Eastmancolor). *ed* — Jan Troell. 12 mins.

DEN GAMLA KVARNEN (The Old Mill)
p — Jan Troell 1962. *sc* — Jan Troell. *ph* — Jan Troell (Eastmancolor). *ed* — Jan Troell. 12 mins.

PORTRÄTT AV ÅSA (Portrait of Åsa)
p — Jan Troell 1963. *sc* — Jan Troell. *ph* — Jan Troell. *ed* — Jan Troell. *l.p* — Åsa Ljunger.

JOHAN EKBERG
p — Sparfrämjandet. *p.c* — Filmkontakt 1964. *sc* — Jan Troell. *ph* — Jan Troell. *sd* — Olle Jacobsson. *m* — Erik Nordgren. *ed* — Jan Troell. *l.p* — Johan Ekberg, Ulla Rodhe. 23 mins.

UPPEHÅLL I MYRLANDET (Stopover in the Marshland)
p.c — Svensk Filmindustri 1965. *p* — Bengt Forslund. *sc* — Bengt Forslund, Jan Troell, from a short story of Eyvind Johnson. *ph* — Jan Troell. *m* — Erik Nordgren. *ed* — Jan Troell. *l.p* — Max von Sydow, Allan Edwall.

Feature Films

HÄR HAR DU DITT LIV (Here Is Your Life)
p.c — Svensk Filmindustri 1965-66. *p* — Bengt Forslund. *sc* — Bengt Forslund, Jan Troell, from the "Romanen om Olof" by Eyvind Johnson. *ph* — Jan Troell. *sd* — Leif Hansen. *m* — Erik Nordgren. *ed* — Jan Troell. *l.p* — Eddie Axberg *Olof*, Gudrun Brost *His Stepmother*, Ulla Akselson *The Mother*, Holger Löwenadler *Kristiansson*, Allan Edwall *August*, Anna Maria Blind *August's Wife*, Max von Sydow *Smålands-Pelle*, Ulf Palme *Larsson*, Jan-Erik Lindqvist *Johansson*, Börje Nyberg *The manager*, Gunnar Björnstrand *Larsson, Owner of the Cinema*, Signe Stade *Maria*, Stig Törnblom *Fredrik*, Åke Fridell *Nicke Larsson*, Ulla Sjöblom *Olivia*, Catarina Edfeldt *Maja*, Bengt Ekerot *Byberg*, Per Oscarsson *Niklas*. 170 mins.

OLE DOLE DOFF (Eeny meeny miny moe/Who Saw Him Die?)
p.c — Svensk Filmindustri 1967. *p* — Bengt Forslund. *sc* — Clas Engström, Bengt Forslund, Jan Troell from Engström's novel "On sjunker" (The Island Is Sinking). *ph* — Jan Troell. *sd* — Lars Lalin. *ed* — Jan Troell. *l.p* — Per Oscarsson *Mårtensson*, Kerstin Tidelius *Gunvor, His Wife*, Ann-Marie Gyllenspetz *Ann-Marie*, Bengt Ekerot *Eriksson*, Per Sjöstrand *Headmaster*, Harriet Forssell *Mrs. Berg*, Georg Oddner *Photographer*, Catarina Edfeldt *Jane*, Bo Malmqvist *Bengt*. 110 mins.

UTVANDRARNA (The Emigrants)
p.c — Svensk Filmindustri 1969-70. *p* — Bengt Forslund. *sc* — Bengt Forslund, Jan Troell from the novels of Vilhelm Moberg. *ph* — Jan Troell (Eastmancolor). *sd* —

Sten Norlén, Eddie Axberg. *m* — Erik Nordgren. *ed* — Jan Troell. *a.d* — P.A. Lundgren. *l.p* — Max von Sydow *Karl Oskar,* Liv Ullmann *Kristina,* Eddie Axberg *Robert,* Pierre Lindstedt *Arvid,* Allan Edwall *Danjel,* Monica Zetterlund *Ulrika,* Hans Alfredson *Jonas Petter,* Ulla Smidje *Inga-lena, Daniel's Wife,* Agneta Prytz *Fina Kajsa,* Halvar Björk *Anders Månsson, Her Son,* Eva-Lena Zetterlund *Elin, Ulrika's daughter,* Åke Fridell *Aron from Nybacken.* 191 mins.

NYBYGGARNA (The New Land)
p.c — Svensk Filmindustri 1970-71. *p* — Bengt Forslund. *sc* — Bengt Forslund, Jan Troell from the novels of Vilhelm Moberg. *ph* — Jan Troell (Eastmancolor). *sd* — Sten Norlén, Eddie Axberg. *m* — Bengt Ernryd. *ed* — Jan Troell. *a.d* — P.A. Lundgren. *l.p* — Max von Sydow *Karl Oskar,* Liv Ullmann *Kristina,* Eddie Axberg *Robert,* Pierre Lindstedt *Arvid,* Allan Edwall *Danjel,* Monica Zetterlund *Ulrika,* Hans Alfredson *Jonas Peter,* Eva-Lena Zetterlund *Elin, Ulrika's daughter,* Agneta Prytz *Fina-Kajsa,* Halvar Björk *Anders Månsson, Her Son,* Tom C. Fourts *Reverend Jackson,* Peter Lindgren *Samuel Nöjd,* Per Oscarsson *Reverend Törner,* Oscar Ljung *Petrus Olausson,* Karin Nordström-Järegård *Judit, His Wife.* 204 mins.

ZANDY'S BRIDE
p.c — Warner Bros. 1974. *p* — Harvey Matofsky. *sc* — Marc Norman from Lillian Bos Ross's novel "The Stranger." *ph* — Jordan Cronenweth (Technicolor, Panavision). *sd* — Charles Knight. *m* — Michael Franks. *ed* — Gordon Scott. *a.d* — Al Brenner. *l.p* — Gene Hackman *Zandy Allan,* Liv Ullmann *Hannah Lund,* Susan Tyrrell *Maris Cordova,* Eileen Heckart *Ma Allan,* Sam Bottoms *Mel Allan,* Joe Santos *Frank Gallo,* Harry Dean Stanton *Walter Songer,* Frank Cady *Pa Allan,* Bob Simpson *Bill Pincus,* Vivian Gordon *Prostitute,* Alf Kjellin *Man by the River.* 119 mins.

JONAS CORNELL

Born 8/11 1938 in Stockholm. Studied at the University of Stockholm 1959-64, and at the Film School 1964-65 with a view to becoming a director. Has published two novels, "Hindret" 1962 (The Barrier) and "Kall oktober" 1963 (Cold October) and the film script "Som natt och dag" 1969 (Like Night and Day). Active as a film and theatre critic editor of the theatre magazine "Dialog." Active as director at Norbotten's Theatre and since 1969 at the Public Theatre of Stockholm (Stockholms stadsteater). Has directed several TV plays in Sweden and in Denmark.

Short Film
HEJ (Hallo)
p.c — Filmskolan 1965. *sc* — Jonas Cornell. *ph* — Lars Svanberg. *m* — Lasse Werner and his friends. *l.p* — Agneta Ekmanner *She,* Stig Torstensson *He.* 12 mins.

Feature Films
PUSS & KRAM (Hugs & Kisses)
p.c — Sandrews 1967. *p* — Göran Lindgren. *sc* — Jonas Cornell. *ph* — Lars Svanberg. *sd* — Lennart Malmer. *m* — Bengt Ernryd. *ed* — Ingemar Ejve. *l.p* — Sven-Bertil Taube *Max,* Agneta Ekmanner *Eva,* Håkan Serner *John,* Lena Granhagen *Kickan,* Rolf Larsson *Jan,* Ingrid Boström *The Piano Girl,* Carl-Johan Rönn *Photographer,* Rebecka Tarschys *Journalist,* Staffan Kullberg *Lecturer,* Leif Zern *Salesman,* Peter Cornell *Young Man,* Lars Löfström, Johan Löfström, Magnus Ryde, Nino Lindblom, Lars Spangenberg *Children.* 95 mins.

SOM NATT OCH DAG (Like Night and Day)
p.c — Sandrews 1968. *p* — Göran Lindgren. *sc* — Jonas Cornell. *ph* — Lars Svanberg (Eastmancolor). *sd* — Kjell Nicklasson. *m* — Robert Schumann, Made in Sweden. *ed* — Ingemar Ejve. *l.p* — Agneta Ekmanner *Susanne,* Gösta Ekman *Rikard,* Keve Hjelm *Erland,* Claire Wikholm *Claire,* Hans Lannerstedt *Daniel,* Birgitta Valberg *Cecilia,* Gudrun Berg *Karin,* Barbro Hiort af Ornäs *Madeleine,* Ernst Günther *Sture,* Håkan Serner *Gustav,* Göran O. Eriksson *Guide,* Carl Johan De Geer *Klas,* Gudrun Ryman *TV Producer,* Kerstin Eriksdotter *Script-Girl,* 100 mins.

GRISJAKTEN (The Pig Hunt)
p.c — Sandrews/Svenska Filminstitutet 1969. *p* — Göran Lindgren. *sc* — P.C. Jersild, Jonas Cornell, Lars Svanberg from Jersild's novel. *ph* — Lars Svanberg (Eastmancolor). *sd* — Kjell Nicklasson. *m* — Träd, Gräs och Stenar and others. *ed* — Ingemar Ejve. *l.p* — Hans Alfredson *Principal Assistant Secretary Lennart Siljeborg,* Keve Hjelm *Cabinet Minister Siwert Gård,* Ingvar Kjellsom *Captain Gustaf Rosén,* Tord Pettersson *Vetenarinary John Blenheim-*

Alskog, Ann-Marie Gyllenspetz *Margareta Siljeborg,* Dan Sjögren *Engineer Karl-Erik Kling,* Bertil Anderberg *Director Thorne-Löwe,* Åke Lindström *Sergeant Heller,* Margit Carlquist *Maud Blenheim-Alskog,* Henrik Allgén, Anna Malmsjö, Peter Malmsjö *Siljeborg's Children,* Folke Walder *Grandfather,* Börje Mellvig *Doctor Schmolze,* Carl Billquist *The Representative.* 94 mins.

JAN HALLDOFF

Born 4/9 1936 in Stockholm. After school he worked as a press-photographer. Still-photographer with Vilgot Sjöman (*491* and *The Dress*) and Jörn Donner (*To Love*). Has directed several TV players and has made entertaining programmes and a youth series for TV.

Short Films
HÅLTIMME
p.c — Svensk Filmindustri 1964. *p* — Bengt Forslund. *sc* — Jan Halldoff. *ph* — Jan Halldoff. *ed* — Jan Halldoff. *m* — Lars Färnlöf. *l.p.* — Karin Stenbäck, Bo Halldoff. 12 mins. mins.

NILSSON
p.c — Svensk Filmindustri 1964. *p* — Bengt Forslund. *sc* — Jan Halldoff from a short story by Stig Claesson. *ph* — Jan Halldoff. *ed* Jan Halldoff. *l.p* — Gösta Ekman *Nilsson.* 15 mins.

BAJEN
p.c — Svensk Filmindustri 1970. *p* — Jan Halldoff. *sc* — Jan Halldoff. *ph* — Hasse Seiden. *ed* — Jan Halldoff. *l.p* — Hammarby IF.

Feature Films
MYTEN (The Myth)
p.c — Svensk Filmindustri/Sandrews/Svenska Filminstitutet 1965-66. *p* — Bengt Forslund. *sc* — Stig Claesson. *ph* — Curt Persson. *sd* — Olle Unnerstad. *m* — Lars Färnlöff. *ed* — Ingemar Ejve. *l.p* — Per Myrberg *Holgersson,* Evabritt Strandberg *Majken,* Naima Wifstrand *Mrs. von Grün,* Bengt Ekerot *Policeman, Social Worker, Doctor.* Per Oscarsson *The Visitor,* Bengt Eklund *The Supporter,* Ulf Johansson *Boman,* Carl-Olof Alm *Blom,* Bo Andersson *Ström,* Berth Söderlund *Socialworker.* 80 mins.

LIVET ÄR STENKUL (Life Is Just Great)
p.c — Svensk Filmindustri 1966. *p* — Bengt Forslund. *sc* — Stig Claesson, Jan Halldoff. *ph* — Curt Persson, Peter Fischer. *sd* — Leif Hansen. *m* — Fabulous Four. *ed* — Wic'Kjellin. *l.p* — Inger Taube *Britt,* Mai Nielsen *Maj,* Keve Hjelm *Roland,* Bengt Ekerot *The Neighbour,* Lars Hansson *Kent,* Thomas Jansson *Thomas,* Stig Törnblom *Jan,* Hanny Schedin *Grandmother,* Leif Carlsson *Little Roland,* Lena Hansson *The Washed-out Girl.* 84 mins.

OLA & JULIA
p.c — Svensk Filmindustri 1967. *p* — Bengt Forslund. *sc* — Stig Claesson, Bengt Forslund, Jan Halldoff. *ph* — Gunnar Fischer (Eastmancolor). *sd* — Leif Hansen. *m* — Claes af Geijerstam. *ed* — Siv Kanälv. *l.p* — Monica Ekman *Julia,* Ola Hakansson *Ola,* Claes af Geijerstam, Åke Eldsäter, Leif Johansson, Johannes Olsson *The Janglers,* Thomas Jansson *Thomas,* Bengt Ekerot *Max,* Lars Hansson *Lasse,* Lars Lind *Nisse,* Signe Stade *The Sister,* Mai Nielsen *The Fiancée,* Arvid Rundberg *Father,* Curt "Minimal" Åstrom *Porter,* Jan Halldoff *Director of the Record Company.* 88 mins.

KORRIDOREN (The Corridor)
p.c — Svensk Filmindustri 1968. *p* — Bengt Forslund. *sc* — Bengt Bratt, Bengt Forslund, Jan Halldoff. *ph* — Inge Roos (Eastmancolor). *sd* — Olle Unnerstad. *ed* — Siv Kanälv. *l.p* — Per Ragnar *Jan,* Agneta Ekmanner *Kerstin, His Wife,* Ann Norstedt *Maria, His Sister,* Åke Lindström *The Father,* Inga Landgré *The Mother,* Gunnar Biörck *Professor,* Leif Liljeroth *Dr. Forslund,* Lars Amble *Stig,* Pia Rydwall *Maud Widén-Andersson,* Bengt Ekerot *Birger Olsson,* Märta Dorff *Mrs. Olsson,* Tina Hedström *Birger Olsson's Daughter,* Mona Andersson *Lise Granell,* Stig Törnblom *Drug Addict,* Linnea Hillberg *Renée Höglin,* Arne Källerud *Kurt Karlsson,* Christina Lundqvist *Mimmi Ståhl,* Thomas Jansson *Thomas.* 97 mins.

EN DRÖM OM FRIHET (A Dream of Freedom)
p.c — Svensk Filmindustri 1968-69. *p* — Bengt Forslund. *sc* — Jan Halldoff, Bengt Forslund. Consultants — Bengt Bratt, Åke W. Edfeldt, Bo Halldoff, Hans Nestinus, Arvid Rundberg. *ph* — Lars Johnson. *sd* — Tage Sjöborg. *ed* —

Siv Kanälve. *l.p* — Per Ragnar *Jan Henry Ravén,* Stig Tornblöm *Stig Johansson,* Bo Halldoff *Probation Officer,* Ann Nordstedt *Ann,* Elisabeth Nordkvist *Stig's Girlfriend,* Inga-Lill Walfridsson *FNL-Girl,* Gurli Svedlund *Kiosk Woman,* Björn Anderö *TV Reporter,* Åke W. Edfeldt *TV Announcer,* Sten Ardenstam *Motorist.* 87 mins.

RÖTMÅNAD (Dog Days)

p.c — Svensk Filmindustri 1970. *p* — Bengt Forslund. *sc* — Bengt Forslund, Jan Halldoff. *dial, ideas* — Lars Forsell. *ph* — Lars Johnson (Eastmancolor). *sd* — Lennart Engholm. *m* — Lars Färnlöf. *ed* — Siv Kanälv. *l.p* — Ulla Sjöblom *Sally Gustafsson,* Carl-Gustaf Lindstedt *Assar Gustafsson,* Christina Lindberg *Anna-Bella, Their Daughter,* Ernst Günther *Their Neighbour,* Eddie Axberg *Anna-Bella'sBoyfriend,* Ulf Palme *Richard,* Jan Blomberg *Photographer,* Gunnar Lindkvist *Captain,* Curt L. Malmsten *Assessor,* Frej Lindqvist *The Finn,* Carl-Axel Elfving *Priest,* Bo Halldoff *Undertaker.* 110 mins.

FIRMAFESTEN (The Office Party)

p — Inge Ivarson 1972. *sc* — Jan Halldoff, Lars Widding. *ph* — Lars Bjorne, Helena Engelsson (Eastmancolor). *m* — Lars Berghagen, Tommaso Albinoni. *ed* — Wic'Kjellin. *l.p* — Siv Andersson *Berit Nilsson,* Lars Berghagen *Man with the Guitar,* Rolf Bengtsson *Hansson,* Bert Åke Varg *Björn "Nalle" Dahlgren,* Lauritz Falk *Knut Levin,* Lars Amble *Karl-Magnus Stridh,* Diana Kjaer *Gunilla Stag,* Nils Hallberg *Harry Sjöberg,* Christina Carlwind *Siw Schilden,* Bo Halldoff *Mr. Nilsson,* Sissi Kaiser *Cashier,* Caroline Christensen *Mrs. Levin.* 97 mins.

STENANSIKTET (The Stone Face)

p — Inge-Ivarson 1973. *sc* — Bengt Forslund, Jan Halldoff. *ph* — Lars Björne (Eastmancolor). *sd* — Olle Unnerstad. *m* — Gugge Hedrenius. *ed* — Susanne Linnman. *a.d* — P.A. Lundgren. *l.p* — Jan Blomberg *Harry,* Ann-Mari Adamsson-Eklund *Eva,* Annika Levin *Lady,* Per Eklöf *Frank,* Leif Möller *John,* Mari Lundin *Nina,* Mats Robbert *Kent,* Ted Gärdestad *Ted,* Bert-Åke Varg *Singer,* Ewert Granholm *Architect Bergsjö,* Bo Halldoff. 91 mins.

BRÖLLOPET (The Wedding)

p — Inge Ivarson 1973. *sc* — Olle Länsberg, Jan Halldoff. *ph* — Lars Björne (Eastmancolor). *m* — Lars Färhlöf. —

l.p — Beatrice Järegård *Eva Eriksson,* Hans Klinga *Kent Långsjö,* Lars Amble *Bert Svanlund,* Bert Åke Varg *Sten Lääng,* Göthe Grefbo *Ivan Snell, the Priest,* Nils Hallberg *Rudolf Dahlvik,* Sickan Carlsson, Anna-Lisa Ericson, Inga Gill *Aunts,* Sten Ardenstam *Bengt Strid,* Bo Halldoff *Bertram Talk,* Gus Dahlström *Erik Eriksson.* 91 mins.

DET SISTA ÄVENTYRET (The Last Adventure)

p.c — Hasse Seiden Film 1974. *p* — Hasse Seiden. *sc* Jan Halldoff, from the novel by Per Gunnar Evander. *ph* — Hasse Seiden (Eastmancolor). *sd* — Kjell Jansson. *m* — Rachmaninov. *ed* — Peter Falck. *l.p* — Göran Stangertz *Jimmy,* Ann Zacharias *Helfrid,* Marianne Aminoff *Mother,* Tomas Bolme *Dr. Davidson,* Åke Lindström *Headmaster,* Birger Malmsten *Captain No. 1,* Margit Carlquist *Sally,* Berto Marklund *Bruno,* Nils Hallberg *Raymond,* Anne-Sofie Nielsen *Linnéa,* Stig Johansson *Valdemar,* Gösta Krantz *Captain No. 2,* Charlie Elvegård *Sven,* Bo-Ivan *Pettersson Lieutenant,* Kerstin Österlin *Kerstin,* Elisabeth Nordkvist *Anita,* Wallis Grahn *Sister Katarina,* Bengt Sundmark *Kerstin's Father,* Ingrid Backlin *Kerstin's Mother.* 113 mins.

MAI ZETTERLING

Born 24 May 1925 in Västerås. Amateur theatre work. Calle Flygare's theatre school 1941. The Dramatic Theatre's school for actors 1942-45. Engaged at the Dramatic Theatre as an actress 1945-47. To England 1946 and worked as an actress there in films, theatre and TV. Later also American pictures and theatre. Documentaries for English TV, together with her husband David Hughes since 1960. Has written the book "The Cat's Tale" (together with David Hughes) 1965 and the novel "Nattlek" 1966 (Night Games).

Film Roles

Lasse-Maja (Dir. — Gunnar Olsson 1941). *I Killed (Jag dräpte,* dir. — Olof Molander 1943). *Frenzy/Torment (Hets,* dir. — Alf Sjöberg 1944) *Prince Gustaf* (dir. — Schamyl Bauman 1944). *Iris and the Lieutenant* (dir. — Alf Sjöberg 1946). *Frieda* (dir. — Basil Dearden, England 1946). *Music in the Dark (Musik i Mörker,* Ingmar Bergman 1948). *Nu börjar livet* (dir. — Gustaf Molander 1948). *Quartet* (dir. — Ralph Smart 1948). *The Bad Lord Byron* (dir. — David MacDonald 1948). *The Romantic Age* (dir. — Jean Gréville, England 1949). *The Lost People* (dir. — Bernard Knowles, England 1949). *Blackmailed* (dir. — Marc Allégret, England 1950). *The Ringer* (dir. — Guy Hamilton, England 1950). *The Tall Headlines* (dir. — Terence Young, England 1950). *The Desperate Moment* (dir. — Compton Bennet, England 1953). *Knock on Wood* (dir. — Norman Panama/Melvyn Frank, U.S.A. 1954). *A Prize of Gold* (dir. — Mark Robson, U.S.A. 1954). *Dance Little Lady* (dir. — Val Guest, England 1954). *Giftas: Ett Jockhem* (dir. — Anders Henriksson 1956). *Seven Waves Away* (dir. — Richard Sale, U.S.A. 1956). *The Truth About Women* (dir. — Muriel Box, England 1957). *Lek på regnbågen* (dir. — Lars-Erik Kjellgren 1958). *Jetstorm* (d — Cy Endfield, England 1959). *Faces in the Dark* (dir. — David Eady, England 1960). *Picadilly Third Stop* (dir. — Wolf Rilla, England 1960). *Offbeat* (dir. — Cliff Owen, England 1960). *Only Two Can Play* (dir. — Sydney Gilliat, England 1961). *The Main Attraction* (Daniel Petrie, U.S.A. 1962). *The Man Who Finally Died* (dir. — Quentin Lawrence, England 1962). *The Vine Bridge* (dir. — Sven Nykvist 1965).

Short Films

KRIGSLEKEN (The War Game)
p.c — British Lion, England 1961. *p* — Mai Zetterling. *sc* — Mai Zetterling. *ph* — Brian Probyn. *ed* — Paul Davies. *l.p* — Ian Ellis, Joseph Robinson *The Boys.* 14 mins.

DE STARKASTE (The Strongest)
p.c — Wolper Pictures, USA 1973. *p* — David L. Wolper, Stuart Margulies. *sc* — David Hughes. *ph* — Rune Ericson (Eastmancolor). *m* — Henry Mancini. *ed* — Edward Roberts. One section of the Olympics film, *Visions of Eight.*

Feature Films

ÄLSKANDE PAR (Loving Couples)
p.c — Sandrews 1964. *p* — Göran Lindgren. *sc* — Mai Zetterling, David Hughes from Agnes von Krusenstjernas series of novels "Fröknarna von Pahlen." *ph* — Sven Nykvist. *sd* — P O Petterson, Tage Sjöborg. *m* — Roger Wallis. *ed* — Paul Davies. *a.d* — Jan Boleslaw. *l.p* — Harriet Andersson *Agda,* Gunnel Lindblom *Adele,* Gio Petré *Angela,* Gunnar Björnstrand *Jacob Levin,* Inga Landgré *Mrs. Levin,* Anita Björk *Petra,* Jan Malmsjö *Stellan,* Heinz Hopf *Bernhard Landborg,* Eva Dahlbeck *Mrs. Landborg,* Hans Strååt *Thomas,* Bengt Brunskog *Tord,* Frank Sundström *Mr. Landborg,* Margit Carlqvist *Dora Macson,* Toivo Pawlo *Lieutenant Macson,* Åke Grönberg *Man with the Bag of Sweets,* Lissi Alandh *Teacher.* 118 mins.

NATTLEK (Night Games)
p.c — Sandrews 1966. *p* — Göran Lindgren. *sc* — Mai Zetterling, David Hughes. *ph* — Rune Ericson. *m* — Jan Johansson, Georg Riedel and Arne Domnerus's orchestra. *ed* — Paul Davies. *a.d* — Jan Boleslaw. *l.p* — Ingrid Thulin *Irene,* Keve Hjelm *Jan as a Man,* Jörgen Lindström *Jan, 12 years old,* Lena Brundin *Mariana,* Naima Wifstrand *Aunt Astrid,* Monica Zetterlund *Lotten,* Lissi Alandh *Mariana's Friend,* Rune Lindström *Albin,* Lauritz Falk *Bruno,* Christian Bratt *Erland.* 105 mins.

DOKTOR GLAS (Doctor Glas)
p.c — Laterna Film, U.S.A./Danmark 1976. *p* — Mogens Skot-Hansen, Joseph Hardy. *sc* — Mai Zetterling, David Hughes from Hjalmar Söderbergs novel. *ph* — Rune Ericson. *ed* — Wic'Kjellin. *a.d* —Bibi Lindström. *l.p* — Per Oscarsson *Dr. Glas,* Ulf Palme *Reverend Gregorius,* Lone Hertz *Helga Gregorius,* Nils Eklund *Markel,* Bente Dessau *Eva Martens,* Lars Lunoe *Klas Recke,* Bendt Rothe *Birck,* Ingolf David *Clas's Father,* Heller Hertz *Anita,* Jonas Bergström *Friend at the University.* 83 mins.

FLICKORNA (The Girls)
p.c — Sandrews 1968. *p* — Göran Lindgren. *sc* — Mai Zetterling, David Hughes. *ph* — Rune Ericson. *sd* — Bob Allen. *m* — Michael Hurd. *ed* — Wic'Kjellin. *a.d* — Charles Delattre. *l.p* — Bibi Andersson *Liz,* Harriet Andersson *Marianne,* Gunnel Lindblom *Gunilla,* Frank Sundström *Doctor,* Gunnar Björnstrand *Hugo,* Erland Josephson *Carl,* Åke Lindström *Bengt,* Stig Engström *Thommy,* Ulf Palme *Director,* Leif Liljeroth *Director of the Tourist Agency,* Margareta Weivers *His Wife.* 100 mins.

VINCENT THE DUTCHMAN
1971. *sc* — Mai Zetterling, David Hughes. *ph* — John Bulmer (Eastmancolor). *l.p* — Michael Gough *Vincent.* 60 mins.

JOHAN BERGENSTRÅHLE

Born 15 July 1935 in Stockholm. Studied at the University of Stockholm. Student theatre in Stockholm and Lund. Assistant to the Danish director Sam Besekow at the Public theatre in Malmö. Active as a director at the H Municipal Theatre in Uppsala and since 1968 at the H Municipal Theatre in Stockholm. Has also directed several TV plays.

Feature Films
MADE IN SWEDEN

p.c — Svensk Filmindustri 1968. *p* — Bengt Forslund. *sc* — Johan Bergenstråhle, Sven Fagerberg from Fagerberg's novel "Det vitmålade hjärtat." *ph* — Gunnar Fischer (Eastmancolor). *Documentaries* — George Oddner. *sd* — P.O. Prambo, Sten Norlén. *m* — Bengt Ernryd. *ed* — Per-Olof Thisner. *a.d* — Bo Lindgren. *l.p* — Per Myrberg *Jörgen*, Lena Granhagen *Kristina*, Max von Sydow *Magnus Rud*, Ingvar Kjellson *Niklas Hedström*, Fred Hjelm *Jonas Myhre*, Lars Amble *Martin*, Olof Bergström *Grönroos*, Toivo Pawlo *Man at the Races*, Ester Larsson *Kristina's Grandmother*, Irma Gustafsson, Sigvard Olsson, Sigg Ågren *Themselves*. 93 mins.

BALTUTLÄMNINGEN (A Baltic Tragedy)

p.c — Svensk Filmindustri/Svenska Filminstitutet 1970. *p* — Bengt Forslund. *sc* — Per Olov Enquist, Johan Bergenstråhle from Enquist's novel "The Legionaries." *ph* — Staffan Lamm, Petter Davidsson (Eastmancolor). *sd* — Lennart Engholm. *m* — Bengt Ernryd. *ed* — Staffan Lamm. *a.d* — Nisse Skoog. *l.p* — Bo Brundin *Erichfuss*, Yrjö Tähtelä *Lapa*, Knut Blom *Alksnis,* and Kristina Dzilums, Anneli Sauli, Karlis Branke, Austris Grassis, Andris Grinsbergs, Modris Gross, Raimond Krastins, Gunnar Pavuls, Johnny Quants, Bengt Ekerot *The Speaker*. 110 mins.

JAG HETER STELIOS (Foreigners)

p.c — Svenska Filminstitutet 1972. *p* — Staffan Hedqvist. *sc* — Johan Bergenstråhle, Theodor Kallifatides from Kallifatides' novel "Foreigners." *ph* — Petter Davidsson, Walter Hirsch (Eastmancolor). *m* — Bengt Ernryd. *ed* — Lars Hagström. *l.p* — Konstantin Papageorgiou *Stelios,* Anastasios Margetis *Tomas,* Savas Tzanetakis *Kostas,* Andreas Bellis *Dimitris,* Maria Antipa *Maria,* Despina Tomazani *Despina,* Edith Jansson *Matron,* Helena Olofsson *Anita*. 110 mins.

HELLO BABY

p.c — Svenska Filminstitutet 1975. *p* — Bengt Forslund. *sc* — Marie-Louise de Geer-Bergenstråhle in co-operation with Johan Bergenstråhle. *ph* — Staffan Lamm (Eastmancolor). *sd* — Klas Engström. *ed* — Lars Hagström. *a.d* — Carl Johan de Geer. *l.p* — Marie-Louise de Geer-

Bergenstråhle *The Girl,* Malin Gjörup *The Girl as Child,* Toivo Pawlo *Father,* Siw Ericks *Mother,* Håkan Serner *First Husband,* Keve Hjelm *Second Husband,* Anders Ek *Anders Ek,* Fred Hjelm *Assistant Director,* Björn Gustafsson *The Homosexual,* Pierre Fränckel *Art-dealer,* Manne Grunberger *Rabbi,* Mikael Söderberg *Beautiful Boy,* Carin Stridh, Bodil Malmsten *Sisters,* Ulla Sallert *An Actress,* Gerd Hagman *Journalist,* Per Myrberg *Manager,* Britt Edwall *Another Actress.*

ROY ANDERSSON

Born 1943 in Göteborg. After his university studies he worked as a teacher. Active in student theatre, composes and plays music. Attended the Film School/The Dramatic Institute 1967-70. Between his feature films he has produced and directed PR-films.

Short Film
LÖRDAGEN DEN 5.10 (Saturday the 5th of October)

p.c — The Film School 1968. *sc* — Roy Andersson. *ph* — Bertil Rosengren, Petter Davidsson. *sd* — Björn Öberg, Lars Johansson-Gudbrand. *ed* — Roy Andersson. *l.p* — Bernt Hedberg *The Son,* Rose Lagercrantz *His Fiancée,* Ingeborg Mähr *His Mother,* Gunnar Ossiander *Landlord',* Deputy, Curt Ericsson *Kolonistugeägaren,* Sol Britt Pilot *His Wife,* Lars Karlsteen *Kolonistugeägarens Granne,* Margot Tännerus *His Wife,* Eric Hansson *Visitor at the Koloniträdgård,* Stefan Böhm *The Baker.* 50 mins.

Feature Films
DEN VITA SPORTEN (The White Game)

p — Svenska Filminstitutet/Svensk Filmindustri 1969. *p* — Group 13: Roy Andersson, Kalle Boman, Lena Ewert, Sven Fahlén, Staffan Hedqvist, Axel Lohman, Lennart Malmer, Jörgen Persson, Ingela Romare, Inge Roos, Rud Spee, Bo Widerberg, Björn Öberg. 100 mins.

EN KÄRLEKSHISTORIA (A Swedish Love Story)

p.c — Europa Film 1970. *p* — Waldemar Bergendahl. *sc* — Roy Andersson. *ph* — Jörgen Persson (Eastmancolor). *sc* — Owe Svensson. *m* — Björn Isfält. *ed* — Kalle Boman. *l.p* — Rolf Sohlman *Pär,* Ann-Sofie Kylin *Annika,* Bertil Norström *John, Annika's Father,* Margreth Weivers *Elsa, Annika's Mother,* Anita Lindblom *Eva, Annika's Aunt,* Lennart Tellfeldt *Lasse, Pär's Father,* Maud Backéus *Gunhild, Pär's Mother,* Gunnar Ossiander *Pär's Grandfather,* Lennart Tollen *Lennart, Eva's Fiancée,* Verne

Edberg *Uncle Verner,* Wiveka Alexandersson *Grand-mother.* 115 mins.

GILIAP

p.c — Sandrews 1973-74. *p* — Göran Lindgren. *sc* — Roy Andersson. *ph* — John Olsson (Eastmancolor). *sd* — Owe Svensson. *m* — Björn Isfält. *a.d* — Anna Asp, Sören Brunes, Lotta Melanton. *ed* — Kalle Boman. *l.p* — Thommy Berggren *Giliap,* Mona Seilitz *Anna,* Willie Andréason *The Count,* Lars-Lewi Laestadius *The Restaurant-Owner.*

LASSE FORSBERG

Born 31/7 1933 in Göteborg. Cinematographer and TV photographer. Has made documentaries for TV and several TV series and TV plays.

Short Films
SAMTAL (Talk)

p — Lasse Forsberg 1963. *sc, ph, ed* — Lasse Forsberg.

PAPPAS DOCKOR (Daddy's Dolls)

p — Lasse Forsberg 196. *sc,* — *ph,* — *ed* — Lasse Forsberg.

ADDENDA

Since the above Filmographies were compiled, several of the directors mentioned have made further films. They are as follows: Bo Widerberg *Mannen på taket* (*The Man on the Roof*), Vilgot Sjöman *Tabu,* Jan Troell *Bang!,* Jan Halldoff *Polare* (*Buddies*) and *Jack,* Lasse Forsberg *Måndagerna med Fanny* (*Mondays with Fanny*), Kjell Grede *En Dåres försvarstal* (*Diary of a Madman,* for TV), and Mai Zetterling a new film for children.

m — Jan Johansson. *l.p* — Per Lilienberg, Fredrik Lilienberg. 10 mins.

MIN STAD (My Town)

p — Lasse Forsberg 1966. *sc* — Lasse Forsberg, Claes Söderquist. *ph, ed* — Lasse Forsberg.

Feature Film
MISSHANDLINGEN (The Assault)

p — Lasse Forsberg 1969. *sc* — Made during shooting by actors, director and the team in co-operation with various experts. *ph* — Lasse Forsberg. *sd* — Björn Hallberg, Johan Classon. *m* — International Harvest. *ed* Lasse Forsberg. *l.p* — Knut Pettersen *Knut Nilsen,* Björn Granath *Björn,* Berit Persson *Berit,* Björn Canvert *Dir. Hedqvist,* Yngve Bjernstad *Police Inspector,* Staffan Seth *Personunder-sökaren,* Stig Billberg *Stig,* Tom Fahlén *Psychiatrist,* Barbro Printz-Bäcklund *Girl over the Yard,* Hans Hellberg *The Author,* Anita Rune *Psychologist,* Anders Edfeldt *Doctor,* Monica Mörild *Nurse.* 104 mins.

Liv Ullmann and Max von Sydow in THE NEW LAND